LIVING ETHICALLY

Also by Sangharakshita

Books on Buddhism
The Eternal Legacy
A Survey of Buddhism
The Ten Pillars of Buddhism
The Three Jewels

Edited Seminars and Lectures
The Bodhisattva Ideal
Buddha Mind
The Buddha's Noble Eightfold Path
The Buddha's Victory
Buddhism for Today – and Tomorrow
Creative Symbols of Tantric Buddhism
The Drama of Cosmic Enlightenment
The Essence of Zen
A Guide to the Buddhist Path
Human Enlightenment
The Inconceivable Emancipation
Living with Awareness
Living with Kindness
Know Your Mind
The Meaning of Conversion in Buddhism
New Currents in Western Buddhism
Ritual and Devotion in Buddhism
The Taste of Freedom
Tibetan Buddhism: An Introduction
Transforming Self and World
What Is the Dharma?
What Is the Sangha?
Who Is the Buddha?
Wisdom Beyond Words

Essays
Alternative Traditions
Crossing the Stream
Forty-Three Years Ago
From Genesis to the Diamond Sutra
The FWBO and 'Protestant Buddhism'
Going for Refuge
The History of My Going for Refuge
The Priceless Jewel
Was the Buddha a Bhikkhu?

Memoirs and Letters
Facing Mount Kanchenjunga
In the Sign of the Golden Wheel
Precious Teachers
Moving Against the Stream
The Rainbow Road
Travel Letters
Through Buddhist Eyes

Art and Poetry
The Call of the Forest and Other Poems
Complete Poems 1941–1994
In the Realm of the Lotus
The Religion of Art

Miscellaneous
Ambedkar and Buddhism
Peace is a Fire
A Stream of Stars

LIVING ETHICALLY

ADVICE FROM NAGARJUNA'S PRECIOUS GARLAND

SANGHARAKSHITA

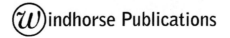
Windhorse Publications

Published by
Windhorse Publications Ltd
169 Mill Road
Cambridge
CB1 3AN
UK

© Sangharakshita 2009

Reprinted with minor corrections 2010, 2011

The right of Sangharakshita to be identified as
the author of this work has been asserted by him in
accordance with the Copyright, Designs and Patents Act 1988

Cover design by Gonçalo Branco
Cover image © absolut
Printed and bound by CPI Group (UK) Ltd, Croydon, CR0 4YY

Jeffrey Hopkins, excerpts from *Nāgārjuna's Precious Garland*:
Buddhist Advice for Living and Liberation. Copyright © 2007.
Reprinted with kind permission of Snow Lion Publications,
www.snowlionpub.com.

British Library Cataloguing in Publication Data
A catalogue record for this book is available from the British Library

ISBN 9781 899579 86 0

contents

about the author

Sangharakshita was born Dennis Lingwood in South London, in 1925. Largely self-educated, he developed an interest in the cultures and philosophies of the East early on, and realized that he was a Buddhist at the age of sixteen.

The Second World War took him, as a conscript, to India, where he stayed on to become the Buddhist monk Sangharakshita. After studying for some years under leading teachers from the major Buddhist traditions, he went on to teach and write extensively. He also played a key part in the revival of Buddhism in India, particularly through his work among followers of Dr B.R. Ambedkar.

After twenty years in India, he returned to England to establish the Friends of the Western Buddhist Order in 1967, and the Western Buddhist Order in 1968. Sangharakshita has always particularly emphasized the decisive significance of commitment in the spiritual life, the paramount value of spiritual friendship and community, the link between religion and art, and the need for a 'new society' supportive of spiritual aspirations and ideals.

In recent years Sangharakshita has been handing on most of his responsibilities to his senior disciples in the Order. From his base in Birmingham, he is now focusing on personal contact with people.

editor's preface

This book owes its existence to the creativity and dedication of a number of people. It is based on material from a seminar given by Sangharakshita in the summer of 1976 on a text from the Mahāyāna Buddhist tradition, Nāgārjuna's *Ratnamālā*, the 'Precious Garland'. Although ostensibly the advice of a great Buddhist teacher to a king, the text is of great value to all Buddhists. Teaching draws out truths, and this is true both of the original text and of the seminar on which this book is based, the participants playing their role, the teacher playing his, and the teaching arising from the interaction between them. The published form of the teaching comes about thanks to the editorial work of Tim Weston, Pabodhana, Jinananda, and Vidyadevi, and many thanks also to Shantavira, for all the care and attention he has given to editing, polishing, and typesetting the text.

The work is to be published in two volumes, of which this is the first. There was too much material for one book, and rather than cutting it drastically, we decided to divide it into two. As is often the way with life, this involved doing something which was also drastic in another way. Nāgārjuna's original teaching investigates and constantly revisits two themes. The first is advice on how to live, encompassing ethics in its broadest, deepest, and most Mahayanistic sense. 'Just as you are intent on thinking of what could be done to help yourself,' Nāgārjuna tells the king, 'So you should be intent on thinking of what could be done to help others,' – and he returns again and again to this theme, both in general and in the specific form of the precepts by which all Buddhists try to live.

But with this first theme, a second is closely entwined. Nāgārjuna says, 'By him who speaks only to help beings [i.e. the Buddha], it was said that they all have arisen from the conception of "I" and are enveloped with the conception of "mine".' Beneath the question of how best to help others, and how to develop the altruistic spirit that wants to, are questions of another kind: what is 'self', what are 'others', and how does a world in which that distinction exists come into being?

For Mahāyāna Buddhism – and no one expresses the vision of that school more fervently and cogently than Nāgārjuna – the practical matter of how to behave in the world is intimately connected with what may seem to us to be much more abstract questions about the nature of existence; and in *The Precious Garland* Nāgārjuna moves easily and continually between the two. When the teaching comes to be discussed by Western students of Buddhism, however, the shifts are not quite so seamless. A discussion which includes the observation that 'people will take pride in almost anything that might bring them a little attention, even if that attention is far from flattering' is very different in nature from a discussion around the point that 'if the existence of something necessarily involves the existence of its opposite, then that thing cannot be said to be absolutely real'.

While from a Mahayanist perspective these two areas of inquiry are intrinsically linked, for the purposes of spiritual practice it may sometimes be useful to separate them; and this is what we have done here. This first volume focuses on what the text has to say about ethics; the second one will concentrate on Nāgārjuna's teachings on emptiness in the same work. Perhaps the second volume could be considered to be revisiting the themes of the first viewed from a different level or perspective. In his recent book, *Precious Teachers*, Sangha-rakshita describes a meeting with a young Tibetan rimpoche. 'I once asked him which picture of the world was correct, the modern scientific one, or the traditional Buddhist one, with its Mount Meru, its four islands, and so on. Both pictures were useful, he replied, but they were useful for different purposes.'

Likewise, perhaps the two views of life and Buddhist practice offered by Nāgārjuna in *The Precious Garland*, the ethical view and the view – or even no-view – of the Perfection of Wisdom are each useful for their own purpose. This book, based on the former, is offered in the hope that it may be useful.

In various senses this is an old teaching: old in the sense, of course, that the original text is centuries old, and old in that the original seminar was held more than thirty years ago. But in a sense it also constitutes a new teaching, in that it contains Sangharakshita's most recent thinking on the subject. He and Samacitta have spent many hours working through the edited text, which was necessary because of his sight problems, but very useful in that in the course of reading the text aloud and listening to its effect, many new insights have emerged and been incorporated within the book. Both report that they have been excited and inspired by their new discoveries.

Vidyadevi
Woonton
Herefordshire
May 2008

INTRODUCTION

The Buddhist monk Nāgārjuna lived some 600 years after the *parinirvāṇa* of the Buddha, in the second or third century CE. For many Buddhists, he is the greatest of the Indian Mahāyāna teachers. An original thinker, he was the author of the *Madhyamaka-kārikā* or 'Verses on the Middle', the foundational text of the Madhyamaka school, besides being the popularizer of the *Prajñāpāramitā* or 'Perfection of Wisdom' scriptures. The work on which this book is based, the *Rāja-parikathā-ratnamālā* or 'Precious Garland of Advice for a King', is one of Nāgārjuna's less well known works. Succinct, comprehensive, and inspiring, it is a masterpiece of Mahāyāna expository literature. It deals with the two definitive, inseparable aspects of the Bodhisattva's life, the Bodhisattva being the ideal Buddhist of the Mahāyāna. These two aspects are the profound Wisdom which realizes the truth of emptiness, and the extensive compassion which engages in activities for the benefit of others. The *Ratnamālā* is, in fact, a Mahāyāna manual, a handbook of the Mahāyāna tradition, and a guide to living in accordance with Mahāyāna principles. The work is

1

addressed to an unnamed king, supposedly one belonging to the South Indian Śātavāhana dynasty.

The *Precious Garland*'s theme is the relationship between the practice of ethics and the attainment of wisdom, and in the course of the work Nāgārjuna explores this relationship from a number of different angles, chiefly in relation to various traditional formulations such as the ten ethical precepts, the six perfections, and the fifty-seven faults to be abandoned. In the course of this exploration he gives the king advice on a whole range of ethical matters, and it is this aspect of his advice to the king on which this book is based. Mahāyāna texts are not perhaps the first works of reference to which a Buddhist seeking advice on ethical matters will naturally turn; among the range of scriptures and commentaries available to us, it may seem more obvious to look to the scriptures of early Buddhism, many of which spell out clearly and uncompromisingly the ethical conduct that supports the seeking of Enlightenment. However, the Mahāyāna has plenty to say on the subject, and although it may seem strange that advice given by a monk to a king nearly two thousand years ago has relevance for modern life, Nāgārjuna's words are in fact extremely useful for anyone seeking to live a Buddhist life today.

The basic principle of ethics, according to the Mahāyāna, is to help others, whereas the view of the Hīnayāna (as Mahayanists called the earlier form of Buddhism) is that the practice of ethics is undertaken largely as an exercise in cultivating and preserving positive mental states. The Mahāyāna does not contradict this viewpoint, but simply regards a wholehearted concern for others as a more positive motivation than a concern for one's own mental states. Another Mahāyāna certainty is that ethical behaviour is grounded in Perfect Wisdom, and at the same time that the development of wisdom is only possible on the basis of an ethical life. That reciprocal relationship is the context, Mahayanists would say, in which the practice of ethics should be considered. It is entirely natural, therefore,

2

that in the *Precious Garland*, Nāgārjuna, that famed exponent of the Perfection of Wisdom, returns again and again to reconsider the basics of ethical life and practice. But before we look at what he has to say on the subject, we could usefully ask how we *know* what he said. Where did these verses come from, and how have they reached us?

ORAL TRANSMISSION AND MODERN SCHOLARSHIP

Whereas the Buddha taught purely by word of mouth, and his teachings were preserved as an oral tradition for 400 years before they were written down in what we now know as the Pāli canon, by Nāgārjuna's time writing was in common use, and Nāgārjuna's work was composed as a literary text, a short work addressed to a particular individual in the form of a letter. Nāgārjuna wrote in Sanskrit, but the text on which this commentary is based is a translation from the Tibetan. This calls for a word of explanation.

> Tibetan Buddhism is essentially the brilliant and complex Buddhism of the Pāla dynasty in north-east India, supplemented by influences from central Asia.

Tibetan Buddhism, which also spread into Mongolia, Sikkim, Bhutan, and Ladakh, is one of three major historical forms of Buddhism that still flourish today, the others being south-east Asian Buddhism (found in Sri Lanka, Burma, Thailand, Cambodia, and Laos) and Sino-Japanese Buddhism (found in Korea and Vietnam as well as China and Japan). Each of these forms is a continuation of Indian Buddhism from a certain point in the history of its development, which continued until it was wiped out in the land of its birth by Muslim invaders in the twelfth century. Indeed, the prominent position Nāgārjuna's works assume in Tibetan literature is evidence of the continuity between Tibetan Buddhism and its Indian antecedents.

Tibetan Buddhism is essentially the brilliant and complex Buddhism of the Pāla dynasty in north-east India, supplemented by influences from central Asia. The transmission of Buddhism from one country to another was not like taking an artefact from one place to another. Indian Buddhists, moving from the subtropical plains and forests of Bengal and Bihar across the huge barrier of the Himalayas into the icy, windswept tablelands of Tibet, were transporting not an object but their practice and teaching. It was like the migration of a living species which faithfully continues to pass on its defining features from one generation to the next while slowly adapting itself to its new environment, eventually to produce a distinct variant of the original species.

Through its various schools, and through the outstanding personalities of teachers such as Milarepa and Tsongkhapa, Tibetan Buddhism has made original contributions of great value throughout its history, while retaining the essential features of the Indian Mahāyāna. In its monastic organization and teaching, Tibetan Buddhism perpetuates the Sarvāstivāda school of ancient Buddhist India. As regards Tantric practice, it keeps alive the symbolic rituals and esoteric meditations of a hundred different lineages of Indian yogis and adepts, and in the texts it uses, Tibetan Buddhism preserves the scriptures imported from India with a high degree of accuracy. Sanskrit Buddhist manuscripts, where they exist at all, tend to be very corrupt, but Tibetan translations are very faithful to the originals.

In all Buddhist traditions, it is understood that reading a work by oneself does not really count.

There is a further reason to trust the Tibetan translation. Although the text is a literary work, the translation we will be using here is based on an oral transmission, involving not just the passing on of the text but an explanation of it as well. If you read a text just by yourself, it might not yield much meaning, whereas if you are fortunate enough to be introduced to it by a competent teacher, you are likely to gain a deeper insight into what it is about. It is thus customary in Tibetan Buddhism to approach a text by going to a guru or teacher who is able to explain and interpret it in the light of what he knows about your own Buddhist practice. Eventually you may in turn explain the text to your own students, and it is in this way that the essential meaning of the work is passed down the lineage.

If the continuity of the lineage is interrupted, as sometimes happens, the correct interpretation might even be lost and have to be discovered afresh. In the case of some quite elementary works this is perhaps not so important, but if the work is an abstruse or difficult one, as the present work undoubtedly is in parts, then the correct interpretation of the text becomes very important. In all Buddhist traditions, it is understood that reading a work by oneself does not really count. Prior to my own monastic ordination, for instance, I was asked exactly which texts I had read and studied in conjunction with a teacher, and these were the only texts I was credited with having read in any proper sense. This attitude is inherited from the earliest times, and the *Precious Garland* itself was composed to be studied in this way. It is not written for the uninitiated reader. It is a pithy presentation of the ideas of the Mahāyāna, suitable for oral explanation by a teacher such as Nāgārjuna himself.

But if it is best to depend upon the interpretation of a teacher, what is the role of the scholar in aiding our understanding of a text like this? In any discussion of the development of Buddhist ideas there are, at the very least, two very different viewpoints: that of modern scholarship on the one hand and that of traditional Buddhism on the other. The traditional Indo-Tibetan point of view is that the Mahāyāna teaching was delivered in its fullness, exactly as expressed in the Mahāyāna sūtras, by the Buddha, but that by the time of Nāgārjuna, approximately 700 years after the Buddha's death, it had disappeared from view, and had to be revived, and in some cases rediscovered, by the Mādhyamika and Yogācāra masters. From the point of view of modern scholarship, however, the Buddha could not have taught the Mahāyāna sūtras, certainly not in the form in which they have come down to us. Perhaps certain things he said and certain teachings he gave contained the seeds that later developed into the Mahāyāna, but the modern scholar would regard Nāgārjuna as having cultivated those seeds and produced from them something that was not previously envisaged. They would not accept the claim of the Mahāyāna that Nāgārjuna was simply the reviver of teachings that had already blossomed in the original dispensation of a Buddha.

These two views are obviously in conflict, but that is not to say that one is right and the other is wrong. The middle way is to give appropriate weight to each view. Clearly it is not possible to accept that the Mahāyāna sūtras were taught by the Buddha exactly as they have come down to us. At the same time, it is important to affirm that they do fully reflect the spirit of the Buddha's original teaching, albeit recast in another form at a later time. We can certainly see in the Pāli texts not only seeds but quite definite statements of teachings that come out more fully later on in the Mahāyāna tradition.

This difficulty arises when one is studying any Buddhist text, even the suttas of the Pāli canon, which Theravādin Buddhists traditionally claim to be literally the word of the Buddha. It is seldom easy to tell, even with these, to what extent they can be regarded as the actual words of the Buddha and to what extent they are later reshapings of his original message. In all likelihood, texts like the *Udāna* or the *Sutta-Nipāta* come as close as anything in the Buddhist canon to telling us what the Buddha said and how he said it, but works whose literary forms reveal that they originated later may reflect the spirit of the Buddha's teaching just as faithfully. There is a very fine line to be drawn between the spirit of the teaching and the letter, and while scholarship is very helpful in any examination of the 'letter' of the text as a text, the guidance of a teacher will bring us closer to the spiritual meaning of that text. This is a process that takes place whenever someone who has realized the spirit of the teaching is engaged in trying to pass on that teaching. Thus in the *Precious Garland* we could say that Nāgārjuna is cultivating seeds that are already present in the *Perfection of Wisdom* (*Prajñāpāramitā*) *sūtras* and the *Sūtra on the Ten Stages* (*Daśabhūmika*) for the benefit of his audience, the king, and giving a new form to the essential spirit of these teachings. In studying classics of Tibetan Buddhist literature such as Nāgārjuna's *Precious Garland*, we therefore come a good deal closer to the mainstream of Indian Mahāyāna doctrine and practice than we might at first have thought.

REASONS TO BE ETHICAL

We can take it that the words ascribed to Nāgārjuna are indeed his, and that the *Precious Garland* gives us an authentic account of the communication between teacher and royal student. Needless to say, there is no royal road to perfect wisdom; the text soon makes it clear that, like anyone else, the king will need to pay attention to his ethical life if he is to become truly wise. Living ethically is essentially about developing compassion, and compassion, in the eyes of Mahāyāna Buddhism, is coordinate with wisdom, wisdom and compassion being the two wings by means of which the bird of Enlightenment can fly. As well as giving the king a great deal of specific advice about *how* to live ethically, Nāgārjuna makes various suggestions as to *why* one should do so. These are scattered throughout the *Precious Garland*, as though at various points the king needs to be encouraged or provoked into greater efforts. Nāgārjuna uses a combination of carrots and sticks: on the one hand, he points out that ethical behaviour is the basis of wisdom and that skilful action leads to happiness, whether in this life or the next; on the other hand, he issues sober warnings about the impermanence of life and about the serious consequences of unskilful actions. Skilful behaviour is thus shown to be the road to a wise and happy life and also the way to avoid pain and misery. What follows is a brief survey of Nāgārjuna's reflections on the necessity of ethical living, and the nature of its rewards.

ETHICS AS THE BASIS OF WISDOM

O King, I will explain practices solely virtuous
To generate in you the doctrine,
For the practices will be established
In a vessel of the excellent doctrine.[1]

The central idea expressed here is that ethical practice is the basis upon which wisdom may be developed. Nāgārjuna lays out his aims, which are not to impart doctrinal information but to plant seeds of the Dharma, the Buddha's teaching. The word 'doctrine' perhaps suggests something that is understood intellectually, but the Dharma is to be realized in every fibre of one's being. Nāgārjuna's organic metaphor – 'generate' – reflects this deeper meaning. It suggests that what he is going to say is intended to spark off something that will become the king's own realization, something that will be brought to birth within him, something that will live and thrive.

> The Buddha did not speak about the Dharma,
> but simply spoke Dharma.

In other words, Nāgārjuna proposes to generate in the king not merely an understanding of the Dharma, but the Dharma itself, just as the Buddha did not speak *about* the Dharma, but simply spoke Dharma. Nāgārjuna doesn't want merely to talk *about* the truth. He wants to *awaken* the king to the truth. He is reminding the king of his inherent potential to attain

Enlightenment, to establish the practices and to become thereby a vessel of the Dharma.

When Nāgārjuna speaks of the 'excellent doctrine' in the fourth line, the addition of an adjective is not just to fill up the verse line. In ancient Buddhist literature, especially verse, every word or syllable contributes to the meaning. He therefore refers to something slightly different from just 'doctrine' on its own, which appears in the second line. In the second line the Dharma is the fruit of solely – or simply – virtuous practices. This Dharma is real enough, it is a living spiritual principle, a practical realization of what is skilful and what is unskilful; but it can be practised even by a beginner. We can assume that the king did not know very much Dharma, if any at all. As a result, Nāgārjuna begins by speaking about morality. He wants to inspire the king, to spark off a more positive state of mind. The term translated as 'excellent doctrine', however, is *saddharma*, which means the true or real Dharma, the ultimate Dharma, the Dharma that is directly concerned with reality. Nāgārjuna foresees that as the king becomes established in the moral practices he takes up, he will become receptive to the Dharma at a significantly higher level.

When people first become interested in the spiritual life, they are not necessarily looking for profound philosophical teachings, or, even if they are, these may not be what it is most useful for them to hear. To begin with, they need something that will give them a feeling for states of mind more positive than the ones they usually experience. They don't need facts and figures about the history of Buddhism. They don't need requests for donations. Nāgārjuna therefore does not burden the king with a discussion of the finer points of the Abhidharma or of Mahāyāna philosophy – at least not yet – nor does he bother his wealthy and influential student with requests for funds with which to build monasteries. If he cannot inspire the king from the start, he might as well save himself the trouble of trying to teach him anything, let alone the 'excellent doctrine'.

Nāgārjuna's 'vessel of the excellent doctrine' is a description of a practitioner of the Dharma. Another teacher compares the four different kinds of disciple to four kinds of pot. The first kind is like a pot that is turned upside down; he or she is completely unreceptive. The second is like a pot with holes in the bottom. Just as whatever you pour into the pot leaks away, likewise, whatever is communicated to this sort of disciple goes in one ear and out the other. They might seem to understand at the time, but nothing is retained long enough to make any real impression. The next kind of disciple is like a pot containing poison, full of negative mental states like resentment, craving, and cynicism. Such a disciple will corrupt and distort the teaching in such a way as to make it harmful to themselves and to others. Finally, there is the disciple who is like a pot that is clean, intact, and empty, ready to receive the Dharma. This sort of disciple is ready to receive the Dharma. He or she is the 'vessel of the excellent doctrine' of which Nāgārjuna speaks. The king's task is to become such a vessel.

In one who first practises high status
Definite goodness arises later,
For having attained high status
One comes gradually to definite goodness.[2]

High status and definite goodness are important terms within the *Ratnamālā*. 'High status' means a happy, positive, and even prominent situation within conditioned existence. In the context of the Tibetan Wheel of Life,[3] the term means a good rebirth in the human realm or among the gods. It is a goal that tradition often assigns to the laity, especially in Theravāda countries. By observing the precepts, worshipping at stupas, and giving alms and donations to monks, one generates good karma, and thus earns the positive but still mundane fruits of that karma, without necessarily concerning oneself with the ultimate goal of Buddhism. 'Definite goodness', on the other hand, refers to those qualities that make for insight, for liberation from conditioned existence, for *nirvāṇa*.

> If they are to make spiritual progress, it would seem that people need to experience a few unpleasant shocks, just to make them think seriously.

According to Nāgārjuna, one who seeks to lead a spiritual life first improves their position within *saṃsāra* (the round of mundane existence) and then goes on to cultivate 'definite goodness', the urge for liberation. Put like that, what he is saying is obviously true. But does everyone who attains 'high status' necessarily start thinking in terms of 'definite goodness', in the sense of trying to realize the inherently insubstantial and impermanent nature of conditioned existence? No, certainly not. We cannot assume that this higher aspiration will arise automatically as the result of a mere accumulation of *puṇya*, or merit, and the attainment of 'high status'. It will arise only if you start thinking seriously about the unsatisfactory nature of conditioned existence itself – despite your enjoyment of 'high status' within it.

Like many traditional teachings, the *Ratnamālā* is meant for a particular audience. Everyone needs the Dharma to be presented to them in a way that will harness their personal predispositions and energies. Here, Nāgārjuna is addressing a king. The traditional Indian belief was that if you were born into a royal family, it was on account of previous good karma. Nāgārjuna is in effect saying that since, as a result of his previous virtuous deeds, the king has attained 'high status', he should now think of achieving or developing 'definite goodness'. He is presenting this as the next natural step, the only real option for a sensible person. The king's merits having gained for him the highest status it is possible to achieve in life, he seems to be saying, there is really only one further step for him to take.

11

Once you assume that a certain course of events will naturally follow from what you are doing now, it will often be those very events that take place. If you have made up your mind about the course before you, there can be a sense of inevitability about it, even though you have to continue to make an effort in that direction. Nāgārjuna is perhaps trying to encourage the king, and to persuade him that his achievement of 'high status' is just the foundation for this decisive step on the spiritual path.

This example of skilful means should not blind us to the fact that in reality there is no summit to human felicity. There is no point at which you will be sure to say to yourself, 'Well, I've come as far as one can get in this world. Now for something of an entirely different nature.' There is, that is to say, no end to human craving. One never feels that one has enough. Even a man who has contrived to bring a whole nation under his control might well want to extend his power still further. If they are to make spiritual progress, it would seem that people need to experience a few unpleasant shocks, just to make them think seriously. If things are going along smoothly you might start taking everything for granted and become unmindful of the impermanence and fragility of human existence, in which case your 'high status' would not have helped you progress towards the goal at all.

This is a subject to which Nāgārjuna turns later in the text:

Always considering that impermanence
Of life, health, and dominion,
You thereby will make intense effort
Solely at the practices.

Seeing that death is certain
And that, having died, you suffer from ill deeds,
You should not commit ill deeds
Though there might be temporary pleasure.

Sometimes no horror is seen
And sometimes it is.
If there is comfort in one,
Why do you have no fear for the other?[4]

If the promise of happiness is not incentive enough to practise, consider, says Nāgārjuna, how precarious is our hold
upon life. We assume that we will live out our allotted span of
years, but this is by no means certain. Even in the conditions
of modern life, the possible causes of death are legion, while
the factors keeping us alive are comparatively few, and even
they can become causes of death. Food, for example, keeps us
alive, but there are so many cases, including that of the
Buddha himself, in which it has brought a swift end instead.

> Don't wait until you have more time. Just do it now,
> in the midst of everything else that you have to do.

The fact of impermanence manifests in a thousand different
ways. If we look at life dispassionately and in detail, we can see
the changes almost as they occur. Though these changes may
be quite small, as we get older they add up to a process of increasing physical and mental decline. We are likely to acknowledge this decline sadly and reluctantly, even anxiously, but it
is possible to see it as something from which we can draw
strength and determination. It is even possible to draw inspiration from events that jolt us into greater awareness such as
some sudden change in health or fortunes, or perhaps a brush
with death. In fact we have every reason to take such remind-
ers of impermanence as a spur to spiritual practice. It is obvious that we don't have much time, and that we may lose the
faculties that we now possess. Life will become more difficult
as we get older. In many ways, we who live in advanced
democracies live like kings, but the privileges we enjoy,
especially the freedom and opportunity to practise the
Dharma, may not always be available to us.

As the fact of impermanence reminds us, life is a brief and precious opportunity, an opportunity to be seized with enthusiasm. Don't wait until you have more time. Just do it now, in the midst of everything else that you have to do. The message of impermanence is the message of the Dharma itself. Impermanence is a death sentence, but it is also our hope of freedom from death, if only we can accept its message at the deepest level of our being, and heed its warning. For Nāgārjuna, impermanence does not imply nihilism, the belief that death is the end. In the West, we tend to regard a belief in a future life or lives as reassuring, but such a prospect is not reassuring for Nāgārjuna or for any true Buddhist. The translation 'ill deeds' is perhaps not the happiest, but the message is clear; what Nāgārjuna is saying is: How can you take comfort from the fact that, despite your misdeeds, you appear to enjoy a good life now? You may relax when you see nothing threatening coming upon you in this life, but when you *do* experience the operation of karma, why do you not take it as a warning that you should mend your ways? Here is the paradoxical nature of human self-delusion. We take comfort when we don't see the karmic results of our unskilful actions, but we don't heed the warning when we do.

This, at least, is the traditional message. I would not put it that way myself, however. I would prefer to say that unskilful actions hinder our development as human beings, and therefore undermine our happiness. They certainly undermine the happiness that results from a good conscience. Why sacrifice real happiness for the sake of some transitory pleasure?

An aspect of 'high status' that it is easy to assume is spiritually advantageous, but which is not necessarily so, is the possession of physical and mental health. It might be assumed that if you are physically healthy and active, mentally robust and socially adept, you will necessarily be more receptive to the Dharma. However, being healthy sometimes comes with a sort of beefy and unreflecting insensitivity, while people who are unwell or unsuccessful in worldly terms – even people who are emotionally disturbed – are sometimes more spiritually sensitive and receptive. In other words, 'skilful' in its Buddhist sense is not equivalent to 'healthy'. That is, the criteria of psychological health espoused by psychotherapeutic or psychoanalytic theory do not quite correspond with Buddhist ideas of what constitutes a mentally healthy human being.

> Spiritually skilful mental states can go with an inability to conform to worldly expectations that can render a person virtually unemployable.

For example, a common rule of thumb used to estimate reasonable mental health is the ability to hold down a job, but the possession of spiritually skilful mental states can go with an inability to conform to worldly expectations that can render a person virtually unemployable. It is as if a little insight sets you going against the grain of the world; you might perhaps become a little eccentric, even unstable. Someone who is healthy in the worldly sense might appear to be a likely vessel for the Dharma, but a rather more battered specimen of humanity, even someone straight out of mental hospital or jail, might prove to be much the more successful Dharma practitioner. To be skilful in the Buddhist sense means to act, speak, and think in a way that takes one away from what are traditionally known as the three poisons: craving, hatred, and bewilderment or mental confusion. You may be healthy in the worldly sense, may function very well in society, and be successful and even happy, but unless you have sufficient insight to perceive the ways in which you are affected by the three poisons, you are not healthy in the Buddhist sense.

High status is considered to be happiness,
Definite goodness is liberation,

The quintessence of their means
*Is briefly faith and wisdom.*⁵

Here, Nāgārjuna distinguishes between two ways of thinking.
You can think in terms of gaining happiness, in which case
you are still concerned with the world, or you can think in
terms of gaining liberation. The difference is quite significant.
The worldly-minded person asks, usually unconsciously,
'What will make me happy?' The spiritually-minded person
on the other hand asks, consciously, 'How can I become free?'

If you are a healthy person in the ordinary sense of the word,
you are likely to judge how well you are doing in terms of how
happy you feel. This translates, objectively speaking, into
what Nāgārjuna terms 'high status'. However, happiness is
not a very reliable guideline. If you do something because you
think it will make you happy, the chances are that you will be
disappointed, and in all likelihood your search for ways to be
happy will continue indefinitely. There will never be an
object that can give you the happiness you seek; you will just
go from one thing to another, becoming more and more frustrated, bored, disappointed, dissatisfied, and unhappy. On the
other hand, if you are thinking in terms of 'definite goodness',
you will not worry too much about immediate happiness,
which means, strangely enough, that you are much more
likely to find it. Happiness is a by-product of the quest for
freedom.

Having analysed well
All deeds of body, speech, and mind,
Those who realize what benefits self and others
*And always perform these are wise.*⁶

Nāgārjuna's conception of wisdom as including the realization of 'what benefits self and others' is thoroughly Mahayanist in that it accepts the Bodhisattva ideal with its aim of
Enlightenment for oneself and others. The traditional phrase

is not to be taken too literally, because to an Enlightened one there is ultimately no distinction between self and others, but it is meaningful for the non-Enlightened mind, and helps to break down that distinction on an emotional level. It also makes it absolutely clear that we are not being asked to put our own happiness to one side altogether in our concern for the happiness of others.

> Wanting to be happy ...
> is a natural and healthy human impulse.

One might say that Nāgārjuna's aim in writing this letter to the king is to direct him towards true happiness, as distinct from the transitory happiness of worldly success. But if the quest for happiness is subsequently to be put aside in the transition from seeking 'high status' to seeking 'definite goodness', this does not mean that there is anything wrong with wanting to be happy. It is a natural and healthy human impulse. How can we wish for the happiness of others if we are alienated from our own desire for happiness?

Unfortunately, many of us in the West were given to understand when we were young that it is selfish to want happiness for oneself, and we therefore feel unnecessarily guilty about wanting it. As a result, we can feel guilty even about *being* happy. 'After all,' the perverse logic goes, 'with all my selfish desires for my own happiness, how could I possibly deserve to be happy?' This further produces the still more perverse belief that if we are to make spiritual progress, we will necessarily have to subject ourselves to great suffering. Such a deep-down belief that you are undeserving, even basically wicked, will inhibit your practice of the Dharma from the very beginning.

This unfortunate state of affairs arises partly from our failure to distinguish between happiness and the good on the one hand and what is pleasant on the other. If we are to lead a spiritual life, it is imperative that we distinguish between happiness and pleasure. We have to realize that doing what is good for us is not the same thing as doing what we like or what we enjoy. However, it can sometimes be so difficult to disentangle the two that it is tempting to assume that the good cannot be pleasant, and that the pleasant is bound to do us harm. To avoid following one's blind desires, one may even make it a rule always to follow the advice of others and do what they think is best for one. From this it is only a short step to thinking that one's natural desire to benefit oneself and to be happy is reprehensible.

If you find yourself in this sort of dilemma, it might be best just to do what you enjoy doing, regardless of people's approval or disapproval, and in this way re-establish contact with your feelings. Ideally, we should act spontaneously, with ease and flexibility, rather than acting out of a sense of being hedged in on every side by self-recrimination or out of fear of transgressing some immutable moral law. Having said that, our wider aim should be to reach out beyond our personal happiness towards what is of profounder concern to us, namely, benefiting others. If you succeed in doing this, you are being a true friend to yourself.

HAPPINESS IS BENEFICIAL

Always observe the discipline
Of actions just as it has been explained,
In that way, O glorious one, you will become
The best of authoritative beings upon the earth.

You should always analyse well
Everything before you act,
And through seeing things correctly as they are
Do not put full reliance on others.

Through these practices your realm will be happy,
A broad canopy of fame

Will rise in all directions,
And your officials will respect you fully.

The causes of death are many,
Those of staying alive are few,
These too can become causes of death,
Therefore always perform the practices.

If you always perform thus the practices,
The mental happiness which arises
In the world and in yourself
Is most favourable.

Through the practices you will sleep happily
And will awaken happily.
Because your inner nature will be without defect,
Even your dreams will be happy.

Intent on serving your parents,
Respectful to the principals of your lineage,
Using your resources well, patient, generous,
With kindly speech, without divisiveness, and truthful.

Through performing such discipline for one lifetime
You will become a monarch of gods
Whereupon even more so you will be a monarch of gods.
Therefore observe such practices.[7]

Here, Nāgārjuna is suggesting to the king that having obtained the acme of worldly power, prosperity, and happiness (through having performed virtuous deeds in previous lives), his next step is to become king of the gods, through further virtuous deeds in this life. As king of the gods he will be in a position of still greater influence, of course. One has only to think of Brahmā Sahampati[8] urging the Buddha to teach the Dharma to get some idea of what kind of influence that might be.

> Happiness is not only good in itself,
> but produces further positive results.

One of the fruits of spiritual practice is clarity, seeing things just as they are. Less coloured by self-interest and personal predicaments, one's views are more objective and one has less need to rely on the views of others for a kind of second-hand objectivity. The other major fruit is happiness. Nāgārjuna's reminder that happiness is beneficial may seem an obvious point, but it is one that is little regarded. Happiness is not only good in itself, but produces further positive results. If you can make people a little happier, cheer them up a bit, there is that much more positive energy moving around. To say, 'Even your dreams will be happy,' seems to be a common way, in Indian literature, of talking about exceptional good fortune.

Through faith you will not be without leisure,
Through good ethics you will move in good transmigrations,
Through becoming familiar with emptiness
You will attain detachment from all phenomena.[9]

The results to be looked for are not necessarily experienced in this life. If in this life you have faith, you will have leisure – presumably for hearing the Dharma – in the next. So why does Nāgārjuna make a connection between faith and having leisure? The point is that if you have faith in the Dharma you will make the best use of whatever opportunities you have to practise it here and now, as you are aware how precious those opportunities are. In fact you will do whatever you can to increase them. The word 'leisure' should not be taken too literally. Among the traditional list of eight conditions of non-leisure, along with various more obviously unsatisfactory rebirths, is rebirth as a long-lived god. The holding of wrong views is also mentioned.

The next consequence of skilful behaviour mentioned by Nāgārjuna relates to an important Buddhist teaching. The

20

practice of ethics is the key to a healthy human existence, whether in this life or the next. The connection he goes on to make is in a sense equally obvious. Insight leads to non-attachment. But the idea of being *familiar* with emptiness suggests more than the occasional flash of insight. It suggests something that has sunk in so deep that it has become the way one normally sees things. The question is whether we have to achieve this first, or whether breaking down our attachments in other ways will by itself give us an appreciation of emptiness.

It seems to be a question of freedom versus discipline. Suppose, for instance, that you are very attached to chocolate. You can either gorge on it until you become sick of chocolate, or you can discipline yourself to give up the indulgence little by little. Both methods work. The insight can arrive either way. But neither method produces insight automatically. Even if you don't give up chocolate, you will in any case need to keep up your practice of reflection and meditation in order to see through the craving. If you give up chocolate as a matter of discipline, on the other hand, you can cut down the craving for it enough to allow you to start to see your habits more clearly. Reducing the craving leaves you freer to examine it. Discipline tends to simplify your life, it gives you more energy, and it helps to maintain morale and momentum. If a number of individuals undertake the same discipline and support one another in it, that also strengthens the *sangha*, as the Buddhist community is called. However, while discipline certainly makes insight more likely through its attenuating of craving, no amount of discipline is a substitute for seeing into the true nature of your craving, which is that it is the cause of suffering.

Crucially, discipline enables you to see the workings of your mind and get a sense of how you would get on if you didn't indulge that particular desire. If you were to fast for three days, say, you would see how your mind works without the physical and emotional support of food. You would see how you feel about food, what it means to you. It's like a laboratory experiment. You take away a certain factor in your life so that you can see what happens when that factor is not present. You don't have to guess. You actually see and feel the result, and as a consequence you know yourself better.

You might then want to make a vow. A vow is very simply a statement – usually a public statement – to the effect that you will do, or not do, something either for a certain period of time, or for ever. Not that you'll try to, not that you promise to: you *will*. When you make the vow it is already accomplished, and there is no question of your breaking it. To make the vow is to keep it. Even if you don't say it in front of other people, you say it in front of the Buddhas and Bodhisattvas, and you call upon them to witness your vow. Having done that, there is no going back, so that when you make a vow you need to know what you are doing and why. For example, you should know yourself well enough not to make a vow out of self-hatred, just as a way of making life difficult for yourself, although even if you did this, you would still have to keep the vow. Should you break a vow, it means you didn't really make it in the first place, and this will show that you are not an emotionally integrated person.

To make a vow presupposes a certain degree of integration. But if you haven't got that when you make the vow, one of the purposes of the vow is to make you become integrated in the course of its fulfilment. In fact, you become more integrated even as you bring yourself to the point of making it. Without being integrated you won't be able to observe the vow, and as there is no question of your not observing it, you just have to become integrated. There's no other way.

THE FOLLY OF UNSKILFUL ACTION

Desisting from all non-virtues
And always engaging in virtues

With body, speech, and mind –
These are called the three forms of practice.

Through these practices one is freed from becoming
A hell-being, hungry ghost, or animal.
Reborn as a human or god one gains
Extensive happiness, fortune, and dominion.[10]

The states of being of the denizens of hell, of hungry ghosts (*pretas*), and of animals are usually designated the 'three downward paths'. It is axiomatic not only for traditional Buddhism but for Indian culture generally that the performance of virtuous actions raises one in the scale of conditioned existence and increases one's happiness and well-being. In other words, virtue pays, in the form of what the translation calls 'high status'. It is very much the Indian belief that a life of virtue will not only raise the level of your consciousness but also produce mundane rewards in the form of a rebirth in which you will have a pleasant and happy time, in which you will be rich, good-looking, and so on. In most Buddhist countries, lay people observe the precepts largely for this reason.

> Taken too literally or carried too far, this attitude towards the practice of ethics becomes what Swami Vivekananda once called a shopkeepers' religion.

I personally doubt whether karma operates quite so straightforwardly as that. In any case, the attitude of measuring the morality of actions by how far they are going to advance you in this world or the next is hardly a spiritual one. It is no more spiritual to think in terms of being reborn in a heaven realm than it is to want to be rich and successful in the present life. Both are inadequate solutions to the problem of human suffering. A utilitarian belief in karma is, at best, an incentive to moral action for people who are only able to think in very materialistic terms. No doubt this is an important consideration; if people are encouraged to behave well out of

23

concern for their own well-being in a future life, it's a good beginning. But we need to be weaned off any dependency on that kind of incentive, for it inevitably compromises the purity of the intention behind moral action, and thus also compromises the spiritual effectiveness of that action.

Taken too literally or carried too far, this attitude towards the practice of ethics becomes what Swami Vivekananda once called a shopkeepers' religion – a trading of good deeds for future worldly benefits. You might even find yourself calculating, for example, that having built up a nice surplus of moral credit you could well afford to backslide in a certain area of your ethical practice. Such naive spiritual materialism is unlikely to attract many people these days. The only people who would be motivated by it would probably be those involved in religious movements that interpret worldly prosperity as a sign of God's approval, or which promise the joys of heaven to the virtuous believer.

The only truly spiritual measure of moral actions is whether or not they lead to *nirvāṇa*, or at least contribute to the basis upon which *nirvāṇa* is attained: that is, whether or not they are performed out of a conscious concern for others as well as for oneself. Another way of putting this is simply to say that a truly virtuous action is its own reward. What better incentive for cultivating a generous, open state of mind than knowing it will lead to even more positive states, and ultimately to Enlightenment? If your skilful states of mind result in wealth and prosperity, there is no harm done, but such material rewards can only be a by-product of truly skilful behaviour, not its *raison d'être*.

How could those with senseless, deviant minds
On a path to bad transmigrations,
Wretched, intent on deceiving others,
Have understood what is meaningful?

How could those intent on deceiving others
Be persons of policy?
Through it they themselves will be cheated
In many thousands of births.

Even if you seek to harm an enemy,
You should remove your own defects and cultivate good qualities.
Through that you will help yourself,
And the enemy will be displeased.[11]

These verses expose the sheer pointlessness of unskilful activities of body, speech, and mind. Such activities cut us off from any possibility of mental clarity. Not only do we create suffering for ourselves; we lose our way, we lose sight of the path away from suffering. We lose any clear sense of our own good, of what is truly meaningful. In cheating others, one cheats oneself in a way that outweighs any possible advantage that may be derived from deceit. Again, of course, it is very difficult to see this when one is dominated by a deceitful mindset. What is worse, it means that one is a stranger to the highly positive experience of unlimited and universal loving-kindness, known in the Buddhist tradition as *mettā* (Pāli) or *maitrī* (Sanskrit).

The advice in the third of these verses seems quite cynical, coming as it does from a great Buddhist philosopher, but we have to remember that it is given with the king's royal responsibilities in mind. A king may have enemies in the sense of enemies of the state, without anything really personal being involved, and he will have to deal with such political foes effectively, even have to prevail over them, without doing them more harm than was necessary. The principle seems straightforward: even if your motivation is impure and you want to get the better of someone, you are still obliged to be considerate. It will benefit you, karmically speaking, as well as influencing the way others view you, and it will discomfort your opponents if they have to revise their opinion of you.

St Paul says something similar: by being kind to your enemy you 'heap coals of fire on his head'.[12]

From non-virtues come all sufferings
And likewise all bad transmigrations,
From virtues, all happy transmigrations
And the pleasures of all lives.[13]

Some Buddhists believe that all our sufferings are due to mis-deeds committed in previous lives, so we have to be quite careful about how we understand Nāgārjuna's assertions here. It is not that all our sufferings are the direct result of un-skilful actions on our part. Certainly an unskilful action will sooner or later be followed by suffering for the person who performs it, but this is not to say that if something unpleasant befalls us, it must be because of our previous unskilful actions. The fact is that sometimes we do feel that we suffer quite undeservedly, and the Buddhist view is that this feeling may be justified. Some of our experience is the result of karma, but some of it is the result of conditions of another kind.

What we *can* say is that all our suffering is *indirectly* the result of our past unskilful volitions. If we take the long view, we find that it is our own thoughts, words, and deeds that have brought us rebirth in the human realm. It is our own mental attitudes that have brought us into conditioned existence, and conditioned existence means suffering. The misfortunes we experience, often through no fault of our own, are an integral part of the mode of being within which our consciousness arose. The way Śāntideva puts it in the *Bodhicaryāvatāra* is that if someone beats you, they must bear the responsibility for taking up the stick, but you must bear the responsibility for having taken up the body that is beaten. It is your own deluded consciousness that has brought about rebirth in the human realm where such things as this may well happen.

YOU AND THE WORLD

Thus observe the practices incessantly
And abandon those counter to them.
If you and the world wish to attain
Unparalleled enlightenment,

Its roots are the altruistic aspiration to enlightenment
Firm like the monarch of mountains,
Compassion reaching to all quarters,
And wisdom not relying on duality.[14]

As we have seen, there are all kinds of traditional incentives and warnings relating to the connection between ethical conduct and one's own happiness and well-being, but of course it is just as important – especially for the Mahāyāna – to consider the welfare of others. Nāgārjuna now puts before the king the Mahāyāna ideal, that is, the Bodhisattva ideal. This ideal is the attainment of 'unparalleled enlightenment', and its 'roots' are the three factors that will help bring this about. The first of these is 'the altruistic aspiration', which is the *bodhicitta*, the wish to attain Enlightenment for the benefit of all beings. This sublime aspiration is so imbued with a sense of the transcendental, and at the same time so deeply interwoven with one's everyday life, that it is unshakeable. The second root is compassion that is without boundaries, that does not falter under any circumstances, whatever the provocation. The third is wisdom that is ungraspable, that gives the ego no foothold.

You should cause the assembling
Of the religious and the worldly
Through giving, speaking pleasantly,
Purposeful behaviour, and concordant behaviour.[15]

Much of Nāgārjuna's advice to the king is offered in terms of the traditional ethical formula of the ten precepts, and that is the basis of the following sections of this book. However,

27

Nāgārjuna also refers briefly to another traditional list, the *saṃgrahavastus*, the four 'means of unification' by which the Bodhisattva brings people together to work for the common enterprise of creating, mythically speaking, a Pure Land.

> Reality is not a comfortable experience for the ego.

Firstly, giving or generosity is the way in which we connect, in the most practical manner, with others. We let go of our tight grip on what belongs to us, whether material goods, money, time, or energy. That which expresses our possessiveness is transformed into a means of expressing its complete opposite. No doubt the recipient is pleased to receive what we give, but more important is the sense of care and concern that any such gesture communicates. Above all, we give the Dharma. We don't distinguish between our personal practice of the Dharma and our communication of it to others.

The second of the *saṃgrahavastus* is affectionate speech. As we shall later see in greater detail, right speech is greatly emphasized in Buddhism. It is not just a matter of the content of our communication; much of our communication is conveyed in our tone of voice, which often reflects our true feelings much more accurately than what we are actually saying. At the same time, it is more difficult to monitor this feature of our speech, because it is much closer to a true communication of ourselves. By the same token, however, if we consciously cultivate affectionate speech, this can change us at quite a deep level.

The third means of unification is beneficial activity. This is not just a matter of helping others; it is also a matter of knowing what would be of most benefit to them, as well as understanding how best to employ one's energy. After all, there is a lot to be done, and one's energy is limited. What would benefit people most of all, at the deepest level, is helping them to access their own energy, by sparking them off, getting them going, inspiring them in some way.

The fourth *saṃgrahavastu* is exemplification, or practising what one preaches. The Dharma is a teaching that has to be realized in daily life, and it is in this way that it is truly communicated. Do we exemplify the qualities that we are asking others to develop? If not, and if there is a discrepancy between the way we are and the way we aspire to be, clearly something is lacking. What is lacking is not so much the ability to be other than we are at present but the courage to be honest about where we really stand. If we can do this, even though it is quite difficult or humiliating to admit our deficiencies – to ourselves, let alone to others – then we are already making great progress. After all, reality is not a comfortable experience for the ego.

In the *Precious Garland*, the *saṃgrahavastus* are part of Nāgārjuna's guidance to a king, not a Bodhisattva, and in fact these practices are relevant at every stage of one's spiritual development. They embody the fundamental virtues of generosity, gentleness, helpfulness, and authenticity, and they can be cultivated in all sorts of ordinary ways.

THE TEN PRECEPTS

Not killing, not stealing,
Forsaking the mates of others,
Refraining completely from false,
Divisive, harsh, and senseless speech,

Thoroughly forsaking covetousness, harmful intent,
And the views of Nihilists –
These are the ten gleaming paths of action;
Their opposites are dark.[16]

In these two verses, Nāgārjuna introduces the precepts on which his advice to the king is mainly based. Seeking to make the point that the basis of wisdom is ethics, he spells out, in the clearest terms, what an ethical life involves. These verses refer to the ten traditional vows or precepts, the *daśa-kuśala-karma-pathas* or 'ten ways of skilful action'.[17] A precept is a training principle, a guideline to ethical behaviour in a certain area of life. The importance of observing the precepts consists not in 'obeying the rules' or in 'being good', but in cultivating skilful ways of being and behaving for their own sake. In that respect, there is always more to do. You throw yourself wholeheartedly into your ethical practice but you are aware at the same time that you may sometimes backslide, at least to a degree. If that happens, you have to begin again from where you left off and try not to indulge in guilty self-recrimination.

> These precepts make up a path of practice rather than being a list of fixed rules or rigid prohibitions.

These precepts make up a path of practice rather than being a list of fixed rules or rigid prohibitions. An ethical precept isn't an absolute in the sense of being something you are either observing or not observing. As long as one is living with the precepts in mind, one's practice could always be worse and always be better. There is always further to fall, and always further to go. The precepts are therefore weightier than our limited experience of them usually allows us to realize. A potential problem is that the notion of precepts as 'training principles' might cause us to feel, consciously or uncon-sciously, that we are being 'let off the hook' a little. One might say to oneself, 'Well, perhaps I'm a bit lax in my attempts to be a vegetarian, but one of these days I'm going to do something about it.'… 'Speech? Well, I'm afraid little white lies are a necessary part of doing business, and it's obvious that a little fruity language helps to get your point across. But perhaps when I get into a management position.'… 'Yes, of course I could be more scrupulous in the way I administer the petty cash – if only I could get away with paying a little less tax.'…

'You know, I'm only getting drunk twice a week now that I'm no longer working behind the bar, so I'm in a much better state of mind most of the time.'…

Of course, this is a caricature, but perhaps not much of one. Although we should be careful not to be too legalistic about observing the precepts, they call for more than a vague intention to behave better in future. We can try, for example, to be more imaginative in the way we approach them, especially by cultivating their positive counterparts: being kinder, more generous, more faithful (in thought and speech as well as in deed), more truthful, more mindful. We can look for new ways in which to express these positive, expansive qualities. As we shall see in the following chapters, the ten precepts deserve considerable thought and reflection; they go far beyond our usual conceptions of ethics.

I

FRIENDSHIP

'NOT KILLING'

In his advice to the king, Nāgārjuna speaks of this precept simply as 'not killing'. But the first precept as usually formulated, 'I undertake to abstain from taking life,' entails much more than that. In Pāli (in which ancient language it is still chanted by many Buddhists), the precept is *pāṇātipātā veramaṇī sikkhāpadaṃ samādiyāmi*. *Pāṇa* means a living (literally a breathing) being, *atipāta* means 'harming', 'assaulting' or 'attacking', *veramaṇī*, means 'abstain from', *sikkhāpadaṃ* is literally 'step in training', and *samādiyāmi* may be rendered as 'I undertake'. The whole precept is thus 'I undertake the step in training of abstaining from harming living beings.'

> It is easy to assume we know what is best for others,
> but we very rarely do know.

The most harmful thing one can do to living beings is to deprive them of life, and in the case of animals this is our main area of concern. When it comes to human beings, however, undertaking simply to refrain from killing them presents a rather perfunctory nod in the direction of the precept. Harming human beings is not only a matter of depriving them of life, or of inflicting pain and suffering. It includes preventing them from realizing their potential, preventing them from evolving and developing as true individuals. (How far animals are able to develop it is hard to say, but it is certainly possible to rob them of the continued enjoyment of their existence.)

The precept is phrased negatively because it is very difficult actively to help another person to grow. If you are able to do so, well and good, but the least one can do is not hinder their efforts to raise and expand their consciousness. The precept could thus be construed as saying: respect the individuality of others; don't get in the way of their positive development.

Some people it is impossible to hinder in this way. They might be prevented from meditating, or even be shut up in prison, but nothing that was done to them would be able to hinder their development as an individual. However, the development of the vast majority of people is much less definite and assured, and it is easily blocked or derailed by the actions, well-meaning or otherwise, of others. It is easy to assume we know what is best for others, but we very rarely do know. The most we can do for others is to provide them with the best possible conditions in which to find their own way, and allow them to make, if necessary, their own mistakes. People need freedom if they are to grow. If we can contribute to that, we certainly should. Apart from that, we should, generally speaking, leave well alone.

FEAR AND POWER

To hunt game is a horrible
Cause of a short life,
Fear, suffering, and hell,
Therefore always steadfastly keep from killing.

33

Those who frighten embodied beings
When they encounter them are malevolent
Like a snake spitting poison,
Its body completely stained with impurity.[18]

In these verses Nāgārjuna warns the king against hunting, which in most cultures has been regarded as a royal pursuit. It was a pursuit that required control over a large tract of territory, provided quasi-military recreation, and enabled the king to display his horsemanship and his tactical skills. At the same time, hunting represented a throwback to the day-to-day conflict with other species in which our Paleolithic ancestors were involved before the introduction of agriculture and animal husbandry. Besides being an aristocratic training for war, it enabled men to experience their primitive instinctual nature, with its craving for excitement and violence. There was also the desire to eat the vanquished creature, thus ingesting its power. Above all, it was probably hunting that originally determined the power structure within Paleolithic tribes, at least so far as the males were concerned. It might have been quite difficult for an ancient Indian king to give up the pursuit without jeopardizing his authority.

> Extreme fear can lead to a disintegration of our sense
> of self, and even cause us to abandon cherished
> personal values in the face of a threat to one's life.

Nāgārjuna is no doubt aware of all this, but he still considers it necessary to warn his patron of the spiritual dangers of succumbing to the lure of the hunt. It was necessary for our ancestors to hunt for food, and it is still necessary for some tribal peoples to do so today. But when there is no need to hunt for food, then hunting, however much one rationalizes, is chasing and killing for pleasure, to satisfy bloodlust, and that is a thoroughly unskilful breach of the first precept.

34

Frightening others is one of the ways in which people make themselves feel powerful, and unlike hunting it is an exercise of power to which almost anyone can be tempted. It is notable in this regard that one of the forms of giving practised by the Bodhisattva, along with the giving of the Dharma, is the giving of fearlessness. To inspire terror in others could be considered as unskilful as the giving of fearlessness is skilful.

In ancient times, fear was perhaps a more common emotional reaction than it is today. There were then many immediate threats to be faced from which people are nowadays protected. We are therefore less inclined to regard giving way to fear as being reprehensible than were those who lived in more heroic ages. As a society we have less need for the kind of physical courage which in the past provided the community with protection. Nonetheless, extreme fear can still lead to a disintegration of our sense of self, and even cause us to abandon cherished personal values in the face of a threat to one's life. To instil fear in others is therefore highly unskilful.

Like desire, fear can be a positive thing. Just as we should have a healthy desire to change ourselves for the better, so we should also have a healthy fear of anything that holds us back from following the path of spiritual development and self-transcendence. Many of us are lulled by our day-to-day routine into a false sense of security, but human existence is uncertain. We are going to die and it is not morbid to be mindful of the fact. We should be 'afraid' of conditioned existence itself.

But fear on behalf of the ego is an unskilful mental state. It is a contraction, even a petrification of energy, and it is therefore unskilful to induce such fear in others. Nāgārjuna himself evokes a deliberately frightful image to make his point. Be frightened of being frightening, he seems to be saying. The result of trying to terrify others will be truly terrifying.

Fear is a primitive animal emotion, like lust and hatred, and it is noticeable how much of popular culture is designed to feed these emotions. Three genres of popular films, for example, cater for our need to titillate ourselves with these emotions: pornographic films, violent films, and horror films. Even the act of inducing a pleasurable thrill of horror, while not as unskilful as inducing hatred or lust, is mildly unskilful for the same reason.

In public life, political and journalistic doom-mongers continually warn us about weapons of mass destruction, terrorism, environmental pollution, over-population, global warming, the effects of passive smoking, the dangers of not wearing a cycle helmet, and so on. Many of their warnings relate to real dangers and reflect a genuine concern for people, and it is certainly a good thing to awaken a concern for the welfare of others, including the welfare of generations to come, jolting us out of any tendency to live for today in a narrow, deluded, and self-indulgent way. However, the motivation of those who deliberately seek to disturb people must be examined. People can be terrorized by violence or the threat of it, but they can be frightened in much more subtle ways too. It is even possible to relish frightening others under an appearance of concern, and some people do have a taste for this, just as some people have a taste for violence. The bearer of bad news may secretly enjoy having the power to influence others, and may get a kick from seeing the effect of their words. Similarly, there is a sort of dark glee to be derived from making people feel really frightened. Not everyone who comes with dire warnings has at heart the welfare of those they fill with dread. During the Second World War, 'spreading alarm and despondency' was popularly known as being a 'Dismal Jimmy' and it was frowned upon for very good reasons, it being a time of very real danger. Any assessment of a threat should be realistic but positive.

Unfortunately, even those who warn of spiritual perils are not always disinterested. Like some old-time hellfire preachers, they may do so in order to gratify their desire for power. If one puts the fear of God into people not out of concern for their spiritual welfare, but simply to reduce them to abject terror, the better to dominate and control them, such hypocritical behaviour is highly reprehensible.

The Bodhisattva, by contrast, spreads confidence and happiness, as in the following verse.

Just as farmers are gladdened
When a great rain-cloud gathers,
So those who gladden embodied beings
When encountering them are beneficent.[19]

Here, Nāgārjuna is referring to the beginning of the monsoon. Today, farmers in India still scan the skies anxiously for the first monsoon clouds, because if the rains are even a few days late, the harvest will be poor. When the monsoon does arrive on time the farmers are glad indeed. The aspiration to gladden beings, which is central to Buddhism, especially to the Mahāyāna, is an important one. To make people happy, to stimulate positive emotion in them, is one of the principal activities of the Bodhisattva (the Bodhisattva being Mahāyāna Buddhism's ideal Buddhist). This does not mean merely being entertaining. Gladdening all beings does not involve anything frivolous; it means arousing genuine joy, in the sense of helping people overcome their deepest fears and anxieties, and awakening them to the truth of the Dharma.

The most important qualities for a Bodhisattva,
and for anyone whose life involves teaching or leading
fellow Buddhists, are inspiration and mettā.

This is the opposite of making oneself feel more powerful. It is not about trying to control others for your own purposes.

37

You are like the rain cloud, giving people what they want and need in order to be truly happy. Like the rain cloud, you open up and give yourself. A significant implication of this is that the aspiring Bodhisattva has a duty to be joyful. You can't gladden others if you are not glad yourself. If you want others to be happy, in more than a theoretical sense, if you want to *do* something about making them happy, then you need to be emotionally positive yourself. If you're a wet blanket, if you're a prophet of doom and disaster, if you're a Dismal Jimmy, then you're hardly en route to becoming a Bodhisattva.

So, if you are looking for Buddhist teaching, follow the joy. A Buddhist centre or community should have a happy, friendly, and peaceful atmosphere. The most important qualities for a Bodhisattva, and for anyone whose life involves teaching or leading fellow Buddhists, are inspiration and *mettā*. If you cannot name the seven *bodhyaṅgas*, for example, that does not matter so much. But you cannot do without inspiration and *mettā*, and these need to be cultivated. Inspiration can be developed through the performance of puja (worship) and through the cultivation of spiritual friendship. *Mettā* is generated through the *mettā bhāvanā*, in which you develop a heartfelt desire for the welfare first of yourself, then of a dear friend, next of someone about whom you feel neutral, and fourthly of someone you dislike, before finally developing an equal concern for all four people and eventually for all beings everywhere. No practice is more supportive of the observance of the first precept, or of the aspiration to live in accordance with the Bodhisattva ideal.

PRACTISING THE METTĀ BHĀVANĀ

The *mettā bhāvanā* is a key Buddhist practice. *Mettā* means responding positively and with warmth to people regardless of their attitude towards oneself. You don't need to practise the other *brahma vihāras*, *karuṇā* (compassion), *muditā* (sympathetic joy) and *upekṣā* (equanimity) separately, in order to respond in this way, though you might sometimes want to explore them within the context of your own meditation. However, you need to understand that the other three *brahma vihāras* are all based on a foundation of *mettā*. If you are unable to practise the *mettā bhāvanā*, and you don't feel kindly disposed, either to yourself or to others, practising any of the other *brahma vihāras* is out of the question. Should you try to generate compassion on its own, for example, without a solid basis of *mettā*, you will squeeze out only a kind of sentimental pity or a horrified anxiety. Or take *upekṣā*. Without *mettā* it is just indifference. As one of the *brahma vihāras*, *upekṣā* arises when you develop the same feeling of *mettā* towards all living beings, as in the last stage of the *mettā bhāvanā*.

It is often the psychologically weaker person
who gets picked on, and I'm afraid this can happen
even within the spiritual community.

Should you feel disinclined to engage in a session of the *mettā bhāvanā*, this will probably be because you are feeling slightly irritable, and want, consciously or unconsciously, to indulge the feeling. So you say to yourself, 'I can't get anywhere with the *mettā* today – I'll do the mindfulness of breathing[20] instead.' But it should be the other way round. The fact that you feel irritated is a very good reason for you to practise the *mettā bhāvanā*, for irritation can often be dispelled by this means. Even if you generally have difficulty with the practice, it is likely that you will still feel the benefit of it – even if the benefit is delayed. You might not be able to generate any *mettā* during the practice itself, or even immediately afterwards, but a shift in your attitude will have occurred.

If you find the first stage of the *mettā bhāvanā* difficult, it is sometimes helpful to start with a stage that you can engage with more easily. I would also suggest spending less time on the first four stages and getting on to the fifth stage more quickly, if you can get your *mettā* flowing more strongly that

39

way. Alternatively, if, as is often the case, you find the second stage the easiest, you can always move from it to cultivating goodwill towards yourself. For example, having found some feeling of goodwill towards a friend, you can imagine yourself in a happy situation with that person, in which each of you is feeling goodwill towards the other. This is how we can kick-start *mettā* towards ourselves. Even if we find it difficult to love ourselves, we usually have to acknowledge that at least somebody loves us.

This experience of being accepted and loved is deeply important to us, and the group exerts control over us by means of the fundamental human need for acceptance. It is terrible to feel rejected by the group to which one belongs, and most people would do anything to get back into a positive relationship with it. We will accept the group's evaluation of us, and reform ourselves accordingly, just in order to be welcomed back into its embrace. Interrogation works in the same kind of way. The person being interrogated is anxious to please someone, anyone: 'Yes, I am a heretic,' 'Yes, I am a spy.' What they are really saying is, 'I will go along with anything you say in order to please you and be accepted.' Only a very strong-minded person can hold out against such extreme pressure.

Even within the sangha or spiritual community we need to be careful not to bring pressure to bear upon anyone by treating them, or labelling them, in an unfavourable way. It is often the psychologically weaker person who gets picked on, and I'm afraid this can happen even within the spiritual community. The pressure may not be perceived as such, and most people would be appalled to think that they were picking on someone, but it is all too easy to find ourselves quietly pushing out of the nest the kind of person who does not appear to be a lot of use, who takes up the community's resources, or who is just different in some way. Mobilizing the united disapproval of the group against any one member can do the latter a lot of damage.

40

Most of us instinctively feel that we could not survive exclusion from the group to which we belong, and in tribal societies this would have been literally the case. Shakespeare expresses the horror of banishment in his play *Richard II*, in which the king exiles two noblemen. Thomas Mowbray, banished for life, leaves England, as he puts it, 'To dwell in solemn shades of endless night'. Henry Bolingbroke announces that, as an exile, he will be able to 'boast of nothing else but that I was a journeyman to grief'. To roam the world as an outsider is bondage; freedom is to belong.

The challenge here is that of not banishing anyone from our concern, not giving up on a person we find difficult. More positively, we all need to offer to other members of the community, especially to those who are not so popular, whatever support and encouragement they need, and express our appreciation and gratitude whenever we can. Many of us experience a degree of self-hatred or self-contempt that makes it difficult for us to receive appreciation at all easily, and an important function of the spiritual community is letting us know that there are people who care for us. This makes it much easier for us to recognize our own good qualities. Some individuals can accept and love themselves regardless of what anybody else thinks and feels about them, but most of us need the approbation of others.

THE FRUITS OF KINDNESS

Even three times a day to offer
Three hundred cooking pots of food
Does not match a portion of the merit
In one instant of love.

Though (through love) you are not liberated
You will attain the eight good qualities of love –
Gods and humans will be friendly,
Even (non-humans) will protect you.

You will have mental pleasures and many [physical] pleasures,
Poison and weapons will not harm you,
Without striving will you attain your aims,
And be reborn in the world of Brahmā.[21]

This is reminiscent of certain verses in chapter 8 of the *Dhammapada*, one of which reads, 'Better than a thousand meaningless verses collected together is one line of verse on hearing which one becomes tranquil.'[22] The difference between them is that the Pāli verses compare Buddhist practices with Vedic ones, whereas Nāgārjuna is comparing one important Buddhist practice with another. He is not suggesting that giving (*dāna*) is meaningless. He believes it to be extremely meaningful, as we shall see. What he is saying here is that love or *mettā* is even more important – more important in the sense of its being primary. *Mettā* comes first. If there is love, *dāna* will naturally follow. But you could, conceivably, offer three hundred cooking pots of food three times daily without feeling much *mettā*. Your motivation might be a desire for merit, or for the praise of others, or for the satisfaction of feeling that you were a particularly generous person.

This verse emphasizes the importance of the mental state over the external action. It is the internal, mental, or spiritual state that really matters and which ultimately determines the ethical status of the external action. Again this brings us back to the *Dhammapada*: 'Experiences are preceded by mind, led by mind, and produced by mind.'[23] Of course, if you act positively, this will affect your state of mind for the better, but unless you make the maintenance of positive mental states your priority, your actions can easily become less ethical.

Mettā is the fundamental positive emotion and the foundation for the development of the *bodhicitta* or 'will to Enlightenment'. Without *mettā* between the members of the spiritual community, there is no possibility of the *bodhicitta* arising in their midst. Ultimately, *mettā* is impersonal, and is without an

42

object, but to begin with it has to be developed in relation to people, and if there are no people around, it is going to be very difficult to develop it. In short, the arising of the *bodhicitta* depends upon there being, within the spiritual community, a palpable sense of *mettā*.

So can one be liberated through love? The short answer is: not on its own. Although it is not emphasized much in present-day Theravāda Buddhism, 'the liberation of the heart through love (*mettā*)', as it is usually translated, appears in the Pāli scriptures in connection with one of two forms or aspects of liberation: *ceto vimutti*, liberation of the mind or heart, and *paññā vimutti*, liberation by wisdom. *Ceto vimutti* is the development of consciousness, of positive mental and emotional states – to the highest possible degree – and this is achieved through *samatha* or 'pacification' practices like the *mettā bhāvanā* and the mindfulness of breathing. The Pāli word *samatha* literally means 'calming down', and it refers to the calming down, the pacification, of all unskilful mental states, and the consequent attainment of the *dhyānas*, states of higher consciousness in which only skilful mental states are present. *Ceto vimutti* represents the complete purification of one's emotional nature; it is a state of intense clarity and positivity. It does not, however, on its own constitute full liberation, for this must include *paññā*, or wisdom, sometimes referred to as *vipassanā*, a term which is especially used to describe the initial flashes of insight. To be liberated by wisdom means to be free from all wrong views, and to have complete insight into the true nature of existence.

Ceto vimutti and *paññā vimutti* are often mentioned together. One who gains Enlightenment is said to be liberated in mind and liberated in wisdom, and thus to have attained *nirvāṇa*. It might be said that the combination of *ceto vimutti* and *paññā vimutti* in the Pāli scriptures corresponds to the combination of *puṇya-sambhāra* and *jñāna-sambhāra* found in the Sanskrit texts of the Mahāyāna. Both pairs of terms refer to the necessity of combining total emotional positivity with complete clarity of vision, and within their respective contexts they both point to the same spiritual fact: that while it is possible to develop these two aspects of the spiritual life separately to a degree, in the end one does need both. One needs both 'collections', that of merit and that of wisdom.

In the case of the Bodhisattva, this balance of qualities becomes *karuṇā* and *prajñā*, compassion and wisdom, and the fact that here it is *karuṇā* that is the complement of wisdom, not *śamatha*, gives us idea of what *śamatha* really means for the Mahāyāna. It isn't just a calming down of unskilful mental states. It is not quietude. When only skilful mental states are present, they are very strongly and actively present. Consequently, one's mind is much more powerful than when it is weighed down by conflicting emotions.

Nāgārjuna is not saying that you cannot be liberated through love. You can be, provided you develop love to such a degree of selflessness that it becomes coordinate with wisdom. What he is saying is that even if your practice of *mettā* does not amount to liberation by love, you will still attain the eight virtues of love. These are: gods will be friendly, humans will be friendly, non-humans will protect you, you will enjoy pleasures of mind, you will have mental and physical pleasures, poison and weapons won't harm you, you will effortlessly attain your aims, and you will be reborn in the world of Brahmā.

The first three of these benefits of practising *mettā* are obvious enough. If you are friendly towards others, others – even non-humans – will be friendly towards you. But does this mean that you will have no enemies? In the case of the Buddha, for example, a mad elephant was sent against him.[24] The Buddha was able to pacify the elephant by virtue of his *mettā*. But who sent the elephant against him? It was his jealous disciple, Devadatta. While even a mad elephant could be affected by the Buddha's *mettā*, a human being who was jealous of him and had resolved to kill him, remained quite impervious to that same *mettā*.

From this we conclude that *mettā* is not an irresistible force such that when we direct it at someone, they have no alternative but to like us. *Mettā* allows people the freedom to reject the *mettā* that is offered. Otherwise it would be an assertion of our will against theirs. *Mettā* is a genuine concern for the well-being of people, whether they like us or not. If we try to use *mettā* to make them like us, this shows a misunderstanding of the nature of *mettā* and we will not succeed. We may start getting irritated and even angry with people because they persist in spurning our so-called *mettā*.

The threat of violence can be extremely frightening, and to respond to it with genuine *mettā*, as the Buddha did on more than one occasion, constitutes a real victory. If you are able to respond in this way, it could have a beneficial effect on the situation. On the other hand, one does occasionally meet people who deliberately behave badly, who have made up their minds to harm one, and who know what they're doing. Such people will not be touched by your friendliness or love. If anything, your warmth will intensify their cold-blooded resolve to hurt you as much as possible. That said, the traditional Buddhist belief is that you can literally deflect weapons and counteract the effects of poison by the sheer force of your own emotional positivity, and perhaps that is so. If you are full of *mettā*, at least you will not draw active hostility upon yourself.

'Without striving will you attain your aims.' In other words, you will attain your aims effortlessly. Things will go more smoothly, more freely, more spontaneously, without the strain of your having to make a willed effort. *Mettā* cannot be forced. If you are powerfully generating *mettā*, you are already in an effortless, positive, and spontaneous state.

45

In this context, the fact that you experience 'mental pleasures and many physical pleasures' can probably be ascribed simply to your being in a positive state of mind. A healthy instinct for pleasure does not need much in the way of external stimuli. Finally, Nāgārjuna says that you will 'be reborn in the world of Brahmā'. The implication is that the practitioner will be reborn in a realm corresponding to the mental or spiritual level attained and stabilized through the experience of *mettā*.

There is a similar list in the *Mettānisaṃsa Sutta:*[25] good sleep, the friendliness of others, protection from violence, ease of concentration, good looks, a lucid death, and a good rebirth. The *Dhammapada* also has such a list.[26] An important theme of all these lists is that *mettā* protects one from arbitrary violence and even from simple accidents. People who are full of hatred are often rather accident-prone. Things seem to go wrong for them, for no apparent reason, and not necessarily as the direct result of their own actions. It is as though they had enemies who were secretly working against them. The root cause of their predicament seems to be self-hatred, even an unconscious need to suffer some kind of punishment. It is difficult to love others if one has no love for oneself, and in that case one will instinctively seek out situations in which one is likely to come to harm or get otherwise into trouble.

People who are positive and cheerful, on the other hand, often seem to lead a charmed existence. They attain their aims easily. It is as though they had friends who were secretly working on their behalf. The root cause of such good fortune seems to be a genuine liking of, and concern for, oneself. It is difficult to hate others if you truly love yourself. And if you feel positively about yourself you are instinctively going to look after yourself and seek out situations in which you will not come to harm.

'BEGET THE PERSON YOU NEED'

If you cause sentient beings to generate
The altruistic aspiration to enlightenment and make it firm,
You will always attain an altruistic aspiration to enlightenment
Firm like the monarch of mountains.[27]

The more you encourage and inspire others to be positive, the more positive you will be yourself, for you are encouraging and inspiring yourself at the same time that you are inspiring them. But you yourself have to be inspired in the first place, at least to an extent, since, otherwise, whatever encouragement you give will only be a matter of words. Your words must express your own genuinely positive feelings if they are to generate feelings in others. Conversely, the response others give you should be inspiring too. This is how communication within the sangha works. It is how the *bodhicitta* may come to arise, and how, having arisen within the sangha, it can be strengthened.

> There's no point in complaining about
> being surrounded by unsympathetic, negative people.
> You must produce the 'man' you need.

There is an anecdote about a Sufi master and his disciple. The disciple had come from far away, and eventually the time came for him to return home. Of course he was sad to go, but not just because he had to leave his old master. He was sad because he would be going back to his own rather unculti-vated people. He said to the master, 'Here I have enjoyed communication of the highest kind, but where I'm going, there won't be anyone I can talk with in this way. I don't know how I'm going to survive. What should I do?' The master replied in his usual laconic way: 'Beget the man you need.' He did not of course mean beget in the literal sense. What he meant was that the disciple should sow seeds of inspiration in

47

the hearts of people and that at least some of them would eventually be able to provide him with the kind of communication he needed.

There is no point in complaining about being surrounded by unsympathetic, negative people. You must produce the 'man' you need. It may look selfish, but it is, at the same time, highly altruistic. It is enlightened self-interest in the true sense, because the man you 'beget' will exist not only for you but also for himself. In fact, he cannot exist for you unless he exists for himself. There is no need to worry about your motivation, for here the whole distinction between selfishness and altruism breaks down. Doing good for yourself, you do good for others. Doing good for others, you do good for yourself.

THE IMPOSSIBILITY OF SACRIFICING YOURSELF FOR OTHERS

Those who despise the Great Vehicle,
Source of all good qualities in that (it teaches) taking delight
Solely in the aims of others due to not looking to one's own,
Consequently burn themselves (in bad transmigrations).[28]

This verse addresses a practical ethical issue. If you express negative opinions, you must take responsibility for the possibility that some people will take what you are saying sufficiently seriously not to get involved with the object of your criticism. This can have a profound effect upon their lives, especially if you have criticized a spiritual tradition. Nāgārjuna goes even further than this. He suggests that because the Mahāyāna is concerned exclusively with the needs of others, criticizing it means that you are in effect preventing others from concerning themselves with *your* needs. On the one hand he appeals to one's narrow self-interest; on the other he presents the Mahāyāna ideal as one of pure altruism, utterly free from self-interest. The latter is the common view of the Mahāyāna, and is not to be taken too literally. It would be more true, if less dramatic, to say that in doing good to others, one is doing good to oneself as well, spiritually speaking. How can you separate the two? When you genuinely sacrifice yourself for others, it is as if something in you at a very deep level of your being, or something outside you with which you feel a deep connection, is being nourished. Conversely, if you sacrifice yourself simply out of self-hatred, or to be 'holier than thou', it is not really for the sake of others at all.

Perhaps this kind of exhortation to ignore or neglect our own needs entirely is to help us overcome our natural selfishness and egocentricity. One may find it more helpful, however, to think in terms of regarding oneself as just one person among many. If you are going to devote yourself to the good of all, that 'all' must surely include you. Otherwise, you are giving yourself a special status. You should include yourself in the same way that you include everybody else, rather than regarding yourself as a special individual whose needs must be sacrificed for the good of humanity.

The Buddhist ideal is often regarded as a selfish one. This can't be because of the concern of the Theravāda to attain individual Enlightenment, for in Christianity there is a similar concern for personal salvation (i.e. for saving one's soul). I think the Western impression of Buddhism as being selfish probably springs much more from the emphasis of Buddhism, as a whole, and of the Theravāda in particular, on - monasticism, and therefore on the necessity of leaving one's home, one's job, and even one's family. One goes forth in search of one's own Enlightenment, leaving others to manage as best they can.

But if you are married, especially if you have children, do you not have a clear duty to stay with them? How can you justify leaving them? Some people are deeply shocked to hear that the Buddha-to-be left his palace, his beautiful wife, and his infant son, and went off into the forest in search of truth. It is not as if he knew for sure that he was going to become

Enlightened and pass on his discovery to countless others down the ages. It was just that he found life deeply unsatisfactory. Well so do a lot of people, but does this mean that they can disregard their responsibilities? On the face of it, the future Buddha's action would seem to be thoroughly selfish.

There is no point in our trying to make excuses for what the young Siddhārtha did in the course of his progress towards Buddhahood. If we argue that he made up for his leaving home by teaching the Dharma to so many people afterwards, we are implying that his leaving was an unskilful action, the unskilfulness of which was subsequently outweighed by his skilful actions. All we really can say in this connection is that in life there are certain situations in which we only apparently have a choice. It is as if you are irresistibly impelled to embark on a certain course of action. You just do what you must do and nobody and nothing can stop you. It is not something you work out, weighing up the pros and cons: you cannot possibly do otherwise. That was clearly the situation in the case of the Buddha-to-be. He just could not stay at home any more, so he didn't.

In reality, however, there is nothing wrong with healthy self-interest. It is undoubtedly true that to be a decent human being one has to consider and act for the welfare of others as well as for one's own welfare. At the same time, it is necessary that one should have a positive attitude towards oneself and one's real needs. Such an attitude is an essential basis for the leading of an effective spiritual life. There is often a degree of cant in the way people speak of the selfishness of those who have chosen a lifestyle that is outside social norms. They are saying, in effect, 'If you do what you want to do, you are being selfish. If I do what I want to do, I am not being selfish.' Siddhārtha wanted to grow and develop, as we might say nowadays, and he felt he couldn't do that at home. It may be that some Buddhists have managed to lead a genuinely spiritual life without leaving home, but in the Buddha's time this would have been difficult. If he was to fulfil his potential as a human being there was only one option before him: to leave home.

The problem is resolved with the arising of the *bodhicitta*. It abolishes the tension between self and not-self. You no longer have to choose between them; there is no more having to balance and adjust the rival claims of self and others. What you do, quite spontaneously, is good for what used to be 'you' and good for what used to be 'others'. When the *bodhicitta* has arisen, you see that in reality there is no self, no other. In a manner of speaking, yes, there is 'me', in which case I must speak as well of 'you', but those distinctions are not to be taken too seriously, as though they were absolutely real, and as though there existed two mutually exclusive entities. Without pressing the analogy too far, or taking it too literally, the Bodhisattva's relationship with all beings is like that of a mother with her baby. The mother doesn't distinguish between her own interests and those of her child. For her, they amount to the same thing. She doesn't think that she needs a rest or a holiday from her baby. On its own instinctual level of attachment, there is the same self-forgetting intensity of love. The difference is that in the case of the mother, her love is an extension of her ego, whereas in the case of the Bodhisattva, it is an extension of his or her non-ego. The mother's love owes its strength to its exclusivity, but the strength of the Bodhisattva's *mettā* and compassion springs from its inclusivity, its universality.

A Tibetan Buddhist story tells how a man once saw a crowd of people and realized that something was happening in their midst. Someone was being given a good beating, he was told, and he could not help feeling sorry for the unknown person. On his pushing his way through the crowd, however, he saw that the person who was being beaten was none other than his own mother, and the sorrow he had previously felt changed at once to a feeling of extreme distress. Almost everyone is like that man. We feel for a few individuals a strong concern that we do not feel for the rest of humanity. The Bodhisattva, however, feels the same wholehearted concern for the welfare of all beings.

RIGHT LIVELIHOOD

The next topic I want to consider is work. Work, or what Nāgārjuna speaks of as 'good livelihood', is a hugely important factor in human life on account of the amount of time we have to devote to it. To this one might add the considerable investment of ego-identity in our work and in how much we earn. The way we spend those eight hours a day, forty-eight weeks a year, for over forty years, will be for most of us the single most significant activity of our lives in terms of its effect on our mental states. Generally, our primary concern is with what we earn from our economic activity and the particular status it confers. However, in the Buddhist context a 'good livelihood' is in many respects the opposite of what the world would see as desirable. A good livelihood is one that does not oblige us to violate the precepts in any way.

> To receive a wage is no compensation for the impoverishing effect of such work on one's mental state.

It has to be admitted that, according to this criterion, there are not many jobs that count as 'good' – or right – livelihood. One rule of thumb is that the simpler the work, the easier it will be to do it while observing the precepts. At the very least our work should not harm anybody. Building work, or cleaning, or some other straightforward physical labour might serve our spiritual needs best, especially in the earlier stages of the spiritual life when we may need to engage with, and integrate, our grosser energies. The early spiritual career of the great Tibetan yogi Milarepa, who was made to build towers and then knock them down over and over again, is an extreme example of this kind of approach, which does seem to work.

On the other hand, if our work holds no real interest for us, this may adversely affect our ability to do it mindfully.

The work to avoid is the kind that is repetitive and boring, that does not engage even your physical energies, and that offers no incentive to improve your performance. Such work drains energy; or rather, you have to use energy to suppress energy while doing this kind of work. To receive a wage is no compensation for the impoverishing effect of such work on one's mental state. Life is too precious to be wasted in this way. As well as doing no harm, our livelihood should ideally benefit ourselves and others. Work that calls for a refined sensibility like gardening or decorating, or work that gives people innocent pleasure, like catering, would do very well, as would the kind of vocational service that involves the direct relief of suffering, like nursing, caring for old people, or some forms of therapy. Work should not violate the first precept, which enjoins non-harming. Nor should one employ another person to do soul-destroying work that one does not want to do oneself, a practice which unfortunately is deeply ingrained in our culture.

> Right livelihood is work that is conducive
> to the realization of our spiritual potential.

Wrong livelihood frequently involves deception of some kind, as when a trader uses false weights and measures. Just as untruthful speech deceives another person, so dishonesty in any business transaction is an abuse of the trust of the other party. But all forms of wrong livelihood involve deception in a deeper sense than that of breaking the precepts. Right livelihood is work that is conducive to the realization of our spiritual potential, but in deceiving others we do harm to ourselves as well as to them.

Some forms of wrong livelihood have unfortunate consequences for society at large. Helping to produce weapons of war, for example, is unskilful in the sense that one is enabling others to engage in killing and violence. But besides this it is unskilful in the further sense that one is directly subscribing to the fundamentally wrong view that wars can bring about peace, that killing is sometimes justified, that, in the words of Robespierre's infamous declaration, an omelette cannot be made without breaking eggs. In other words, you have to delude yourself. In order to engage in that kind of livelihood, you have to ignore the fact that a nation is driven to go to war by fear and hatred, however carefully masked by rational arguments those passions may be.

Working as a butcher involves the acceptance of another fundamentally wrong view. In order to pursue this means of livelihood, you must convince yourself that the slaughter of animals and birds is necessary, or at least justifiable. This wrong view finds expression in various ways. First, there is the scientific argument. As omnivores, human beings are natural consumers of animal flesh, so that not to eat meat goes against nature and is probably bad for our health. Asking people to abstain from eating meat is therefore unreasonable. Second, there is the fact that some religions sanction meat-eating, the sanction being based on their belief that the rest of creation exists to provide for the needs of human beings. Third, there is the butcher's own argument: that if he didn't do the work, and in this way support his family, someone else would do it.

These arguments are advanced in support of views that spring from ignorance, fear, and greed. The fact is that if one was not paid to work as a butcher, it is highly unlikely that one would care to be one, and if one was not attached to the taste of meat and to the supposed benefits of a meat diet, one would probably not want to be a meat-eater. If one really looked at what it means to eat meat, one would not be able to consume one's beef and mutton with a good conscience, much less still enjoy them. It would be felt to run counter to all that was truly human in one's nature. Like working for the arms trade, working as a butcher helps create an environment which is not conducive to the well-being of either society or the individual.

Wrong views affect all aspects of life. I once saw an advertisement that read, 'Pregnant? Why not deal with it the sensible way?' and these chilling words were followed simply by a telephone number. But if a woman is planning to have an abortion, she will have to hide from herself the reality of what she is doing, just as those who are engaged in wrong livelihood do. This may well be the only way she will be able to undergo the procedure.

> Right livelihood is work that you would do regardless of how much, or how little, you were paid to do it.

Whatever our livelihood, the way we view it may involve a degree of deception. Work is not always fun. People need money and they don't know how else to get it. If they could, many would like to have the money without having to do the work. Work may indeed be seen as the best way of utilizing human energy, but here too there can be deception. One might even say that any form of wage slavery must involve an element of deception and even self-deception. Can you honestly say you are working if you do not really care about the work? You will be just 'going through the motions'. Things will no doubt get done, but if you are not giving yourself to what you are doing, there will be an element of make-believe involved. If they did not have to work for money, many people would not know what to do with themselves all day. But this in itself reveals the alienating effect of a narrowly utilitarian approach to work, as a result of which it becomes difficult to break out of this attitude in order to do things for their own sake.

We can also see an element of deception in the way that wages are set. The connection between the tasks performed and the reward obtained is really quite arbitrary. Why is one hour's work in the fields worth the price of a pound of rice? Why one pound of rice and not two? On what basis is one hour's work in an office equivalent to ten pounds of rice? The value of work in terms of wages received is largely determined by the vagaries of market forces and the calculations of accountants, even when different people are doing the same work. In any case, what is money? It is essentially a means of exchange, which in former times meant gold and silver coins and which now means banknotes, which have no intrinsic value. Our economic system is based on our all agreeing to treat these objects *as if* they had value. The situation becomes even more obscure when banknotes are replaced by numbers held in computer systems. Of course, quite often the things on which we spend our money have no intrinsic value either. Advertisers and fashion gurus persuade us to purchase articles which are supposed to change our appearance or our home life for the better but which often signally fail to do so.

The solution is to do work that is intrinsically worthwhile. Even work that is difficult, dirty, or unpleasant is nonetheless worth doing to the extent that it contributes to the well-being of oneself and others. Right livelihood is work that you would do regardless of how much, or how little, you were paid to do it. Unfortunately, few people are in a position to enjoy this kind of work.

2

GENEROSITY

Nāgārjuna renders the second precept as 'not stealing'. In Pāli this is *adinnādānā veramaṇī* – 'to abstain from taking the not-given'. It is usually assumed that following this precept means no more than not stealing, not pilfering, not surreptitiously taking what has not been given. Someone might say, 'I've never stolen anything in my life. Well, maybe a fountain pen when I was a kid. Oh, and there was a five pound note I borrowed in a pub. I always meant to give it back the next time I was in there. Apart from that I've never broken the second precept.' But this sort of self-satisfied moral accounting is not the way to practise the precept of giving in its full sense. Like the first precept, the second precept means far more than it appears to mean at first sight. It can also be seen as not hindering a person's development or violating their individuality. You might not take their money or their belongings, but it is very easy to waste someone's time or to rob them of their energy. It is easy to take from someone something other than material possessions that they may be no less sorry to lose. You have not asked, you have simply taken it, and time and energy are things that are not easily given back.

Practising the second precept implies generosity, of course, but it also involves another positive quality: the faith that one way or another you will receive what you need, so that you don't have to take from others against their will or without their permission. Sometimes others will disappoint you; they may forget to look after you in your old age, but your faith has to be a broader confidence in the spiritual and even the psychological rewards of skilful action. Feeling the need to grab your share, to pocket what you feel is yours by right, suggests a neurotic insecurity, as does trying to manipulate events to your own advantage. Any kind of possessiveness, and even the simple tendency to see things and people as commodities, goes against the spirit of this precept. The whole attitude of bargaining, trying to get the best deal for oneself, runs counter to it. The ability to be generous with your skills, your time, and your possessions, without calculating what you are going to get in return, can come only from a state of deep psychological security. You might not get the outcome you envisaged; you might be surprised, whether pleasantly or unpleasantly, at how things turn out; but you will be confident that ultimately there will be a positive outcome for you. The ideal society should function in this way: you give what you can and you take what you need. In the real world the situation is more complex, because there are people who will exploit you if you let them and you may need to drive hard bargains with them. Most people are pretty determined to hang on to what they have, however they may have acquired it, and in seeking to persuade them to let go one must be careful not to resort to methods which break this precept, either in the letter or the spirit.

One way is to appeal to people's natural – if sometimes rather deeply hidden – generosity. This method was pursued with some success in India by Acharya Vinoba Bhave, in his *bhudan* or land-donation programme (*bhu* meaning 'land' and *dan* 'giving'). In India, one of the great social, economic, and political problems is that of the landless labourer. At the same time, there are landowners who have far more land than they really need. The question was how to redistribute this surplus land without having recourse to coercion. Vinoba Bhave, as a follower of Gandhi, was totally committed to the principle of non-violence. His solution was to organize meetings of the big landowners and make the following appeal. He would ask them how many sons they had, between whom they would be dividing their land. They might say five. He would reply, 'So if you had a sixth son, each of the others would have to make do with a little less land,' and they would agree. He would then say, 'Well, take me as your sixth son, and let me have that share.' He didn't get the millions of acres that he had hoped for, but many of the landowners were deeply touched by his appeal and he was able to distribute tens of thousands of acres to landless labourers and their families. This direct approach, with its simple moral appeal, can sometimes work wonders. The beauty of it is that everyone benefits, including the donors. In a politically sensitive situation, motives will often be mixed, and no doubt some owners of land gave out of fear of the consequences of not giving, throwing a sop to the landless in order to reduce popular support for the Communist party. But some experienced a genuine change of heart and gave far more than they were asked to give. In this way, Vinoba Bhave's scheme helped to correct an imbalance in the ownership of land in many parts of India without recourse to violence. It goes to show that encouraging people to be generous doesn't necessarily mean taking advantage of their feelings of guilt. People do sometimes respond positively to a positive appeal. The precepts are not only about ceasing to do evil; they also inspire us to act positively towards others and to encourage them to act likewise.

GIVING AND EARNING

Giving is the fundamental Buddhist virtue. Before taking up any other practice, one should learn to be generous. Many of the *Jātakas*, the stories of the Buddha's previous lives, depict the Buddha-to-be as practising *dāna* or generosity to a superlative degree. As a result, when he is reborn, he has only to open his hands to find them full of jewels – or so the legends relate.

> True generosity … one not only gives all the time;
> one is also aware of receiving all the time.

But is the importance of giving reflected in our own experience of life? What is the real relationship between giving and getting? According to Nāgārjuna, and the Buddhist tradition in general, to be slow to give will result in one being poor, whether in this life or another, while giving freely will lead to wealth. But how are we to interpret this teaching? The first thing to remember is the importance of intention in the creation of karma. It is the spirit in which one gives that counts. But although giving without thought of benefit to oneself will, paradoxically, bring one the greater benefit, most people cannot help opting for the lesser benefit. We can't help thinking of what we will be getting in return, even with regard to such intangibles as esteem, gratitude, and so on. Having a preconceived idea of some sort of quid pro quo means that the gift isn't *really* a gift, and often the recipient will be subtly aware of this. It is usually not difficult to see that much of what we are given comes with various little strings attached. Past experience might make us a bit suspicious of almost any gift, seeing it as 'a sprat to catch a mackerel', as the old saying has it. When one is given something, it doesn't always feel like it, and one might even feel a little disappointed, as though something was missing.

Much of our discontent comes from a sense that life is not fair and that we don't get treated as we deserve; and this in turn may make us unwilling to give. According to the Buddhist view, meanness makes one poor, but meanness itself arises, it could be said, from the fact that one feels poor or has a 'poverty mentality'. True generosity involves the opposite: one not only gives all the time; one is also aware of receiving all the time. Part of the practice of generosity therefore consists in becoming aware of how much one is being given. That is, generosity is connected to the ability to experience gratitude, as well as to express it. It consists in the ability to feel wealthy even in the humblest circumstances.

At the most basic level we have sunlight, air, water, earth. All these are free. We might squander and pollute the elements that we need to live in the world, but they continue to be available to us. Moreover, any advanced society provides all sorts of astonishing services at little or no cost to the consumer. In Britain we have access to so many resources: healthcare and education, libraries, the BBC, all kinds of entertainment, even Buddhist centres. Besides all this, there is the support we are given by those around us. Many people, especially if they are young, are unaware that someone is shopping, cooking, and cleaning for them day after day. There is, for example, the story of the long-suffering housewife who has been cooking for her husband and sons day in, day out, for a quarter of a century with never a word of thanks. One day they lift the lid of the vegetable dish to reveal a pair of old boots. 'Well,' she explains in response to their expressions of shock and dismay, 'You've never said anything that would make me think you'd notice the difference.'

Many people find it difficult to give or receive thanks gracefully. Perhaps they were never introduced to the traditional courtesies, or perhaps they have discarded them as the hypocritical niceties of conventional middle-class life – or perhaps they just feel embarrassed. If one is a bit clumsy in this respect, there is no harm in working on one's social skills. It is always better to err on the side of excess in expressing gratitude. Practice, after all, makes perfect. On the other hand, there are situations where thanks in the formal sense would be out of place. Often, a little look of gratitude will suffice.

If you have energy you will feel like giving.

If we take things for granted we are depriving ourselves of a rich source of satisfaction. This in turn may deprive us of the capacity to give freely, as well as of the further rewards that follow in the form of happiness and free-flowing energy. If we are looking for a return from our generosity, we can find it in the freedom of letting go of possessions, in the natural pleasure we feel in helping someone, in the flow of energy out from us as well as the flow of energy towards us. A psychologically healthy person has energy, and energy naturally flows outwards, so that if you have energy you will feel like giving. Energy flows in different ways, depending upon one's temperament. You might feel like doing something practical for someone, like giving money or time, or you might want to give attention or affection. On the other hand, advice – which most of us are only too willing to offer – is often the one gift that is best withheld.

A friend of mine used to say, 'The greatest virtue is availability.' To be available to others is – quite simply – to be ready to give yourself. You don't insist that you will only help in a particular way. You're not concerned about 'doing your own thing' or 'expressing yourself' or exercising your own talents. You are not too grand for little humdrum jobs. You are simply there for someone or for a certain situation, and you don't mind what you do. This is the ideal of what one might call the 'non-specialized human being'. You are willing to turn your hand to practically anything, and you have no personal investment in the task you happen to be doing. You can see that there is a job to be done and you're happy to do it.

Giving is a kind of communication. In giving, you are opening the channels of communication, and this allows an exchange of energy to take place. Giving, affection, and energy can all flow in either direction. If you are able to give, you are able to receive, and in that sense giving and receiving are two sides of the same coin. A one-way communication can be genuine, but it is necessarily limited. Any interaction between people involves both giving and receiving. Of course, the more intense and the more true the communication, the less it is possible to speak in terms of either giving or receiving. The giving becomes the receiving, the receiving becomes the giving. Who is receiving from whom, and who is giving to whom, it becomes impossible to say.

THE PRACTICE OF GIVING

Just as you are intent on thinking
Of what could be done to help yourself,
So you should be intent on thinking
Of what could be done to help others.

If only for a moment make yourself
Available for the use of others
Just as earth, water, fire, wind, medicine,
And forests (are available to all).

Even during their seventh step
Merit measureless as the sky
Is generated in Bodhisattvas
Whose attitude is to give all wealth away.

If you give to those so seeking
Girls of beauty well adorned,
You will thereby attain
Thorough retention of the excellent doctrine.

Formerly the Subduer provided
Along with every need and so forth

Eighty thousand girls
With all adornments.

Lovingly give to beggars
Various and glittering
Clothes, adornments, perfumes,
Garlands, and enjoyments.

If you provide (facilities)
For those most deprived who lack
The means (to study) the doctrine,
There is no greater gift than that.

Even give poison
To those whom it will help,
But do not give even the best food
To those whom it will not help.

Just as it is said that it will help
To cut off a finger bitten by a snake,
So the Subduer says that if it helps others,
One should even bring (temporary) discomfort.[29]

We all think about our own needs very carefully. But we tend not to think with equal care about what will help others. Even when we are trying to help others, we are only too often self-referential. We would like others to be happy in a way that suits us, or at least matches our ideas of what one should do with one's life. I'm not sure if many people *love* to think about the needs of others, as Nāgārjuna tells the king he should do. We might be able to help others out of a sense of duty, but our aim should be to do so out of love. The first of these verses thus gives us something quite simple and straightforward – and at the same time quite challenging – to aim for in our spiritual life. If we can feel real concern for the needs of others, we will really have made some progress, spiritually speaking.

> He reminds us that we can apply ourselves simply to
> meeting the demands of the present moment.

How should we go about this? Nāgārjuna gives us a clue in the next verse. He says, 'If only for a moment'. We don't necessarily have to commit ourselves permanently to this way of being. He reminds us that we can apply ourselves simply to meeting the demands of the present moment. Make yourself available to others – now, rather than when you feel like doing so. This suggests that it might not be so difficult after all. In a sense, 'making yourself useful' probably covers it. More deeply, it is a matter of radically changing the way we think of ourselves. Instead of looking out at a world made up of resources that could meet our own needs, we can think of ourselves as being a resource for the world.

Many of these verses could have come from the *Bodhicaryāvatāra*, whose author, Śāntideva, lived 500 years after Nāgārjuna and belonged to his spiritual lineage. 'Just as earth, water, fire, wind, medicine, and forests are available to all' inevitably reminds us of the verse from the *Bodhicaryāvatāra* that is recited in the final section of the sevenfold puja.

Just as the earth and other elements
Are serviceable in many ways
To the infinite number of beings
Inhabiting limitless space;
So may I become
That which maintains all beings
Situated throughout space,
So long as all have not attained
To peace.[30]

Nāgārjuna's suggestions as to suitable gifts, like providing beggars with garlands and perfume, and giving girls in marriage to those who seek them, might seem a little odd to us. However, at the time he gave this advice, if you were

65

unable to afford a wife – and therefore were unable to produce children – you would have had no one to support you in your old age. And treating a beggar as you would your dearest friend, giving lovingly rather than with condescension, is a good example of true generosity.

Finally, Nāgārjuna mentions appropriate giving, or giving with a real awareness of the recipient's needs. Sometimes what one gives may even be temporarily unwelcome. Sometimes what someone really wants and needs may be a quite ordinary thing. Sometimes they may even need 'poison' in the form of powerful drugs because they are seriously ill or in pain.

GIVING THE DHARMA

Through making the hearing and the giving
Of the doctrine be unobstructed
You will [keep] company with Buddhas,
And will quickly attain your wishes.

Through non-attachment you will achieve the meaning (of doctrines),
Through not being miserly your resources will increase,
Through not being proud you will become chief (of those respected),
Through enduring the doctrine you will attain retention.[31]

There are two ways in which we can help the communication of the Dharma (that is, the Buddha's teaching): we can help people to teach it, and we can also help people to hear it. Even if we don't give the gift of the Dharma ourselves, we will keep company with the Buddhas if only we do everything we can to enable those who can teach the Dharma to do so, and if we enable those who might be receptive to the Dharma to hear it. This teaching is central to the Mahāyāna approach. To make an effort to help others to benefit from the Dharma is in effect to practise the Dharma yourself. The more you give, the more you receive. I would go so far as to say that you haven't really started practising the Dharma until you have started giving –

above all, until you have started giving the Dharma. The principle of karma applies very directly to our giving of the Dharma: 'through not being miserly your resources will increase'; by being generous with your understanding of the Dharma, you are increasing your own understanding of it.

Until you concern yourself with the needs of others and start giving, you don't realize how attached you are to your own concerns and needs; and until you start teaching it, you don't realize how inadequate is your understanding of the Dharma. When you start teaching, then you really start learning. Teaching opens you up to an entirely different dimension of understanding. While it is inadvisable to start giving people the benefit of your wisdom prematurely – especially if it is mere book-learning – there does come a point beyond which you are going to learn more from teaching than you are from being taught. It is not therefore a question of being 'ready to teach'. You may be less than brilliant as a teacher in the beginning, but by being brought up against the limits of your knowledge, you are forced to grow beyond those limits, both as a teacher and as a student.

You may, for example, be asked about issues that you have shied away from addressing on your own account. Most people have areas about which they feel confident and others that they don't want to look at or are not interested in. Maybe it's some aspect of ethics, or a meditation practice that you have so far neglected. You then have to think about it for yourself, look up texts on the subject, ask your friends about it, and come back with something to discuss with your students. What you come back with may well have a deeper, more significant effect upon you than upon your students. In this way, not only do gaps in your knowledge get filled in, but you may be inspired to investigate further. You may even find you know more than you thought you did.

Of course, you need to have a small stock of Dharma knowledge before you start teaching. It's like going into business.

You need a bit of capital to start with, and some people can make a success of a business with a comparatively small sum. If you think you need a really big sum before you can start, you may not take the plunge at all. In the same way, some people have the ability to start teaching on the basis of quite a small stock of Dharma knowledge, and through teaching they may increase this stock quite rapidly.

The necessary proviso is that you should be honest about what you know and what you don't know, rather than trying to bluff your students by guessing an answer or brushing off difficult questions. You should admit you don't know, or can't remember off hand, and you should look forward to investigating the matter. 'Through not being proud you will become chief of those respected.' The converse of this is that if you try to impress people you may not be respected by them. Nobody can know everything about Buddhism. If you're asked a question that had never occurred to you before, you could say, 'That's interesting. I've never thought about that. What do you think?'

The other thing you need if you are going to teach the Dharma is a certain depth of spiritual practice. People don't want to be given information that they could just as easily find out for themselves. They want live contact with the Dharma, a feeling of how the Dharma is actually lived. They might not be ready to encounter a Buddha, and they are unlikely to find one teaching at a Buddhist centre, but so long as you have assimilated what knowledge you have acquired and have some experience to fall back on, you will be able to communicate something of value. The Dharma can be truly communicated only in the light of a solid practice of it over a period of some years. It isn't an abstract thing. It is not really to be encountered apart from the people who, at least to some extent, actually embody it in their lives. As a Buddhist, you should be turning aspects of the Dharma over in your mind whenever you can, so that if you are asked to teach you already have something to say, perhaps on a subject you have thought about for years. Thus you will always be ready to give a talk or lead a class.

I think we can interpret the second verse quoted here as a continuation of the theme of the first, namely, as being about learning and teaching the Dharma. If you are full of yourself, how can you be receptive? There is a Zen story that illustrates this point. A master called Nan-in once received a visit from a learned professor and poured him tea – and kept pouring until the cup overflowed. When the professor protested, Nan-in replied, 'You are like this cup. How can I give you the teaching when you are so full of your own views?' Learning about the Dharma means learning to listen, not being so attached to one's own views that one is closed to what might be disturbing. This is why the disciple is called a *śrāvaka*, or 'one who hears'.

The self-defeating nature of selfishness is a constant theme of the Mahāyāna. If you are too attached to what is yours, and too full of yourself, you will end up ignorant, poor, and despised. This teaching is traditionally understood in terms of karma and rebirth, viewed as administering as a kind of poetic justice: if you are generous you will be reborn rich, if you are modest you will be reborn into a highly respected position in life. In fact, this is not necessarily the case; as well as karma, there are other factors that determine the nature of our lot in life. Nonetheless, a miser will always feel poor, and those who demand respect will never feel that they are getting enough of it. By contrast, if you are truly generous you are likely to feel that you are living in the midst of abundance, and if you are modest, you will at least enjoy the respect of the few who appreciate modesty.

Karma and rebirth are never a straightforward matter. Selfless actions are one thing, but selfless motivation, especially if you have future lives in mind, is another thing entirely. True selflessness is in the end not separable from insight. For the

69

sake of the greater reward you have to forget all about rewards and just give for the sake of giving. That's the paradox. It's like trying to be happy or trying to love: the more you try to be happy, the less likely you are to be so, and the more you insist on how much you love people, the less likely they are to believe you. But forget all about being happy and loving and you will have a good chance of *being* happy and loving and even perhaps of being loved.

'Enduring the doctrine' is an odd expression, suggesting that the Dharma is a kind of burden, something to be put up with. But that is not what is meant. The term Nāgārjuna uses here is *dharmadhara*, one who bears or carries the Dharma by virtue of their practice of it. Such a person will retain it, that is, they will keep it in mind.

THE BUSINESSMAN'S GUIDE TO PRUDENT GIVING

If you do not make contributions of the wealth
Obtained from former giving to the needy,
Through your ingratitude and attachment
You will not obtain wealth in the future.

Here in the world workers do not carry
Provisions for a journey unpaid,
But lowly beggars, without payment, carry to your future life
(What you give them) multiplied a hundred times.

Always be of exalted mind
And take delight in exalted deeds.
From exalted actions arise
All effects that are exalted.

Create foundations of doctrine, abodes
Of the Three Jewels – fraught with glory and fame –
That lowly kings have not even
Conceived in their minds.

O King, it is preferable not to create
Foundations of doctrine that do not stir
The hairs of wealthy kings
Because (those centres) will not become famous even after your death.

Through your great exaltation, use even all your wealth
Such that the exalted become free from pride,
(The equal) become delighted,
And the inclinations of the lowly are reversed.

Having let go of all possessions,
(At death) powerless you must go elsewhere,
But all that has been used for the doctrine
Precedes you (as good karma).

When all the possessions of a previous monarch
Come under the control of the successor,
Of what use are they then to the former monarch
For practice, happiness, or fame?

Through using wealth there is happiness here in this life,
Through giving there is happiness in the future,
From wasting it without using or giving it away,
There is only misery. How could there be happiness?

Because of lack of power while dying,
You will be unable to make donations by way of your ministers
Who will shamelessly lose affection for you
And will seek to please the new monarch.

Hence while in good health create foundations of doctrine
Immediately with all your wealth,
For you are living amidst the causes of death
Like a lamp standing in a breeze.[32]

This series of arguments in favour of generosity is pitched, it has to be said, at a rather low level. Nāgārjuna clearly thinks that the important thing is to get the stream of generosity flowing. It doesn't matter too much how you go about persuading people to give, just so long as they do give. Giving is a virtue in itself; it frees up energy, it loosens the bonds of some basic unskilful attitudes, and the rest of the spiritual life can be based upon it.

> Never mind karma and rebirth,
> or past and future;
> what is important is how we shape ourselves
> in the present moment.

'Here' means in the present life. If you enjoy wealth now, it comes to you as a result of the generosity you have practised in previous lives. If, therefore, you want to gain wealth in future lives, you must give from your present possessions. To most modern Buddhists, at least in the West, this attitude is at best meaningless and at worst ignoble. But if we are to understand how Buddhism has developed over the centuries, we have to take this traditional way of thinking into account. We have to appreciate that in the past this sort of argument was a real incentive for people. One reason for this must be that life then was much more precarious than it is now. Life was apt to be 'nasty, brutish, and short' for anyone without means. It is therefore hardly surprising that happiness should be so closely allied to the possession of wealth or – as is insisted here – to its profitable expenditure as well. No doubt mundane motivations sometimes fuel our own practice of the Dharma. Are we not often seeking happiness, success, and security for ourselves through such spiritual practice rather than Enlightenment for the benefit of all beings? So perhaps we should not be too censorious of the spiritual materialism of the past. However, to say, 'Lowly beggars, without payment, carry to your future life what you give them multiplied a hundred times' provides an almost grotesque reflection of this traditional, robustly mercenary way of thinking about generosity and its advantages. It envisages a situation in which, in effect, you employ beggars to transport your wealth from your present life to the next.

It may be hard for us to imagine a truly religious-minded person being quite as self-centred as this, but plenty of evidence of such attitudes is to be found in all religions. In India I came across a certain old-fashioned type of devotee belonging to the rich merchant community who would be very pious and very generous, but who would bring his commercial acumen into his religious life. Such a man might make big charitable donations, but he would blatantly attach conditions to them. He would quite shamelessly offer so many lakhs of rupees to open a charitable dispensary, a hospital, or a school, on condition that it should be named after his father, that he himself should be guest of honour at the opening ceremony, and that he should be introduced to the prime minister after he had opened the institution.

This combination of materialism and piety may seem strange to us, but it is ultimately based on traditional religious values. It is bound up with the idea that power and wealth come from one's good deeds in a previous life. It reinforces the notion that the wealthy man is the good man, and with it the notion that the poor man is morally suspect. This is not in fact the Buddhist view, but a rather literal presentation of the teaching of karma and rebirth can unfortunately lend itself to this sort of interpretation. It is, however, the generally accepted Hindu understanding of the teaching, and one that causes the pious and wealthy to feel very satisfied with themselves. I have met many people in India with a firm conviction of their own virtue, born out of little more than their fortunate and prosperous circumstances. And, sadly, I have met many poor people who assumed that they must have deserved their fate. This unpleasant twist, which is sometimes given to the teaching of karma and rebirth, even by some Buddhists, is institutionalized within Hinduism in the form of the caste system and is used to reinforce the social status quo.

Christianity has been put to much the same use in the past. The church regularly taught that it was one's duty to accept one's station in life since it been allotted one by God. There is a hymn in which there appears the following verse:

The rich man in his castle,
The poor man at his gate,
God made them high and lowly
And ordered their estate.

It is as if organized religion tends to sanctify the status quo, and to be on the side of the rich against the poor. As St Paul said, 'The powers that be are ordained of God.'[33] Regardless of how those in power behave, they have God's authority behind them.

In India, I found that rich people often thought of themselves not as exploiters of the poor, but as providers of employment for those who hadn't the brains to create job opportunities for themselves. They genuinely believed that they were performing a public service and amassing wealth quite disinterestedly. It was their way of serving God, they would sometimes say. Such statements used to leave me speechless, but one did come across Buddhist monks who were only too happy to countenance such attitudes.

Throughout his career, the Buddha dealt with the rich and powerful without being in the least deferential. Yet in some Buddhist countries there are monks who will adopt a subservient attitude to those in positions of authority. This is due to a failure to grasp the central principle of the spiritual life, namely, that we are free to choose how to be, here and now, regardless of social and group constraints. We are free to be more or less aware, more or less creative, and more or less of an individual. Never mind karma and rebirth, or past and future; what is important is how we shape ourselves in the present moment. This is the Buddha's own emphasis, that is, the emphasis is on gaining Enlightenment here and now, in this very life. He didn't deny the truth of karma, but he never suggested that a good rebirth was the most worthy goal for a human being. In presenting any Buddhist teaching you have to relate it to that central principle, since otherwise you may be understood as appealing to a lower self-referential motivation.

In justice to Nāgārjuna, one has to bear in mind that in his day a king possessed unlimited power and was capable of doing so much harm that it was worth restraining him by virtually any means. Usually there was no other power within the state by which he might be constrained. If he was not highly intelligent, or religiously minded, one might have to put aside one's scruples in order to encourage some kind of ethical behaviour, however crudely motivated that behaviour might be. One might have to promise him a future life in which he would have more of whatever he had now, if this was the only way of inspiring him to rule ethically.

3

SEXUAL RELATIONSHIPS

The third precept – *kāmesu micchācāra veramaṇī* – is 'to abstain from sexual misconduct'. Forsaking the wives of others (which is how Nāgārjuna refers to this precept) is therefore the very least that a male practitioner of the Dharma should expect from himself. The masculine perspective is here taken as for granted because the text is addressed to a king. Furthermore, in ancient India a man's wife was considered to be his property, and the traditional interpretation of the precept reflects this belief. The precept was also seen as covering abstention from the violation or abduction of any woman, married or unmarried, and this was again in large part a matter of respecting the property of other men, inasmuch as a daughter or sister, however mature, literally 'belonged' to her family until she joined another family through marriage. Until then, she was under the protection of her father and her brothers.

Moving from history to modern practicalities, it is clear how the third precept is to be applied today, whether by women or by men. Two main principles seem to be involved. First, one should not violate another person's individuality by using them for one's sexual gratification against their wishes. Second, inasmuch as someone is regarded as 'belonging' to their sexual partner, knowingly breaking up a marriage or other sexual partnership is a form of 'taking the not-given', as well as being a case of violating the individuality of the person whose partner one has 'stolen'.

But if we limit our sexual activity to what is socially acceptable, can we leave it at that? Is this simple criterion enough? It is, if a rule is all that you want. It isn't, though, if you want to make the observance of the precept a real ethical practice. I once saw the precepts written up on a board in a vihara (Buddhist monastery) in London, and the third one was 'not to indulge in wicked love'. The monks obviously wanted people to think about this precept a bit more deeply. But how does someone practise the third precept if they are married and simply don't have the time or the inclination to indulge in 'wicked love' in any case?

Not to misbehave with other people's partners does not exhaust the implications of this precept. For a start, we should clear away a lot of the rationalizing and romanticizing that serves to idealize, even spiritualize, sexual activity. We like to imagine that sex is all about giving and sharing, but is this really the case? If we are honest with ourselves, can we say that the tremendous attraction we feel towards another person is really just an urge to give? I suspect that in the great majority of cases, sexual relationships are nicely judged reciprocal arrangements, balanced exchanges of services, physical and emotional – healthy enough on their own level, but not to be elevated above that level. Should one try to elevate them in this way, one is inevitably going to be disappointed, or even resentful, when those services are no longer being offered quite so freely, or when they are withdrawn altogether.

Then there is the question of mindfulness. What is the real effect of sexual activity upon one's state of mind? It is worth taking the trouble to notice this if one is attempting to combine a spiritual life with sexual activity. No doubt Tantric adepts and advanced Bodhisattva yogis can incorporate sexual activity into their spiritual practice, but we have to ask ourselves if we are really anywhere near that level. It is not as if an occasional lapse of mindfulness is going to put a stop to our spiritual life. Lapses are inevitable. Even after years of practice, instinctual urges and old tendencies may emerge from time to time and result in a temporary setback in our overall spiritual progress and there is no point in getting caught up in self-recrimination. What is spiritually incapacitating is self-deception.

Furthermore, making allowance for natural drives is not to be confused with the view that a healthy person *needs* sex, and that we are repressed or deprived if we do not get it. Unfortunately the assumption that sexual innocence or purity somehow blocks the healthy functioning of the individual is widely accepted. From this comes the curious idea that one needs to accumulate a lot of worldly experience in the form of personal difficulties and messy sexual relationships to be 'mature' enough to embark upon the spiritual life. There is almost a stigma attached to having to admit that one hasn't had sex for months or years at a time, as though that made one unattractive, a failure, even not quite a real man or a real woman. This is a very pervasive *micchā diṭṭhi* (wrong view) these days. But it is certainly not the traditional view, either in the West or in the East. The mistaken assumption underpinning it is that the same rules can be applied to everyone. But people are different. There are many things that are important to one person but are of no consequence to another. Some people can't live without sex, while others get by quite happily without it, at least so long as they are not constantly being told that they must surely be unhappy. People who are temperamentally inclined to chastity, perhaps as a result of very positive karma, may come to the spiritual life innocent and pure and make considerable progress. Perhaps they have a 'gift' for chastity; if so, they should be allowed to enjoy that gift, not be pushed against the healthy and refined grain of their nature into seeking the kind of experience that most of us feel we cannot live without. Those of us who are not so gifted should allow ourselves an outlet for our sexual urges, without undermining the confidence of those who can practise the Dharma happily without the need for sex. Why not rejoice in purity and innocence as a virtue and a blessing, even if the rest of society takes a completely different view?

The third precept is concerned with what we do with our sexuality in the broadest sense. It is not just about sexual relationships; it is also concerned with how we use our sexuality in order to achieve other objects, as when we charm people in order to get what we want. There is an unpleasant mixture of mutual exploitation and deception in much of what we accept as normal social intercourse between the sexes. This precept is therefore also about being aware of a certain kind of power or energy that is available to us and of the part it plays in the half-conscious flirtation that creeps into so much of our communication. We should respond to people with real friendliness and *mettā*, but not get caught up in the kind of exchange that stirs up sexual feelings in a thoughtless way.

> Sexual feelings cannot be kept in a sealed box
> apart from all one's other emotions.

Along with this unconscious misuse of sexuality, there often goes a fear of experiencing sexual feelings, particularly when those feelings have for their object a person of the same sex as oneself. This is not to say that such feelings have to be acted upon, but sexual feelings cannot be kept in a sealed box apart from all one's other emotions. Our sexuality, for good or ill, seeps into all sorts of situations in which we would nevertheless not want to express it, and the danger is that we become afraid even to acknowledge the presence of this element in our experience. An unconscious fear of experiencing supposedly unacceptable sexual feelings sometimes prevents people from acknowledging and expressing normal feelings of attraction or affection. Being emotionally drawn to someone is automatically identified as a sexual feeling when it might not be anything of the kind. In this way, quite positive feelings can be replaced by emotional unease, by inhibition and, consequently, by loss of energy.

We need to be able to feel strong, warm emotions in connection with our sexuality, but we need also to be able to experience strong, warm emotions without sexual feelings being involved at all. If it is difficult for you to separate such emotions from sex, this doesn't mean that it's a good idea to repress the sexual feelings and take up a life of strict celibacy. Should you do so, those feelings will almost certainly emerge later in life and then be more difficult to handle. Conversely, the more freely we are able to express positive emotion, the better we will be able to deal with our biological or instinctual urges.

THE UGLINESS OF THE CONDITIONED

Lust for a woman mostly comes
From thinking that her body is clean,
But there is nothing clean
In a woman's body in fact.

The abdomen and chest is a vessel
Of feces, urine, lungs, liver, and so forth.
Those who through obscuration do not see
A woman this way, lust for her body.

There is pleasure when a sore is scratched,
But to be without sores is more pleasurable still.
Just so, there are pleasures in worldly desires,
But to be without desires is more pleasurable still.

If you analyse thus, even though
You do not achieve freedom from desire,

Because your desire has lessened
You will not lust for women.[34]

In his advice to the king, Nāgārjuna finds it necessary to devote over twenty verses (only four of which are quoted here)
to curbing the male reader's sexual appetite. Why? Let us first
look at the argument.

> These verses have to be seen as pertaining to method
> rather than to doctrine, the method in this case being that
> of a means to help men overcome their sexual craving.

We are used to washing off all the various secretions and
excretions of our own body, and yet we go into paroxysms of
desire over the unclean body of another. There is something
absurd, Nāgārjuna is suggesting, about such a situation. Similarly, there is a certain intense satisfaction to be gained from
scratching an itching sore, yet no one who knew what it was
like to be free of that terrible itch would willingly have it back.

The majority of teachings of this sort are addressed to men,
but similar views about the body are found in the *Therigāthā*,
the Enlightenment verses of the early Buddhist nuns. The
corresponding reflections recommended for the nuns, to help
wean them from their attachment to men, are less concerned
with the repulsiveness of the body. At that time at least, they
seem to have been attracted less by men's physical attributes
and more by their apparent trustworthiness, so those verses
make much of how treacherous and faithless, how disloyal
and deceitful, men can be; how you cannot trust their sweet
words, how they say one thing and mean another, and how
they will betray your trust even as they gaze lovingly into your
eyes. Their verses focus on the fact that it is the nature of men
to be unfaithful and to lust after other women.

This harsh view of the male sex is probably quite acceptable to
many people today. But the attitude towards woman's body

that we find in the present verses runs right against the grain of modern sensibilities. Probably most people would consider the systematic cultivation of this way of thinking about the female body as morbid, unpleasant, and negative. Looked at superficially, these verses and other Buddhist texts like them may seem to represent a powerfully misogynistic strain running through the Buddhist tradition. They seem to put women down. But they are in fact not intended as an objective assessment of women; they have to be seen as pertaining to method rather than to doctrine, the method in this case being that of a means to help men overcome their sexual craving.

The problems that people have with verses like these stem, I would say, from the quite different nature of the major obstacles faced in the spiritual life by men and by women. These obstacles are more to do with identity than with sex itself. Nowadays men seem to find giving up sex a real problem, representing as this does a loss of an important part of their masculine identity. However, this identity is forged largely by male competitiveness in the workplace, and men probably start to make more real spiritual progress when they wholeheartedly give up worldly ambition rather than when they give up sex.

It would seem that a woman's difficulty with celibacy is also less to do with sex itself and more to do with her identity as a woman. In her case it seems to be more to do with losing the emotional intimacy that goes with sex, and with losing, ultimately, the possibility of her being a wife and mother. The adoption of a celibate lifestyle thus represents for her a tremendous step in itself. The question of children in particular, while it may have become less important for most men than it was in the past, remains comparatively important for women.

CONTEMPLATION OF BODILY IMPURITY

The Sanskrit term to which Nāgārjuna is making reference in these verses is *śubha*, which is here translated as 'clean', while the negative form *aśubha* is translated as 'filthy', although these terms can also be translated as meaning 'pure' and 'impure', or 'lovely' and 'unlovely'.

> Lust can override our natural repugnance for the secretions and excretions of other people's bodies.

Aśubha is often associated with the three *lakṣaṇas* or characteristics of conditioned existence. According to Buddhist teaching, conditioned existence is *duḥkha* (unsatisfactory), *anitya* (impermanent) and *anātman* (without a substantial, unchanging, self). Sometimes *aśubha* is added to this list. When this is done and the four are seen in the opposite way, they become the four *vipariyāsas*, the 'mental perversities' or 'topsy-turvy views'. Being ourselves conditioned, we cannot help ascribing what are in fact the characteristics of the Unconditioned to conditioned existence. We see the world not as unsatisfactory but as *sukha* or pleasant. When we possess things we think we will always have them, that is, we see conditioned existence not as impermanent but as *nitya* or permanent. We also see it not as devoid of permanent unchanging selfhood, but as possessed of such selfhood, or *ātman*. Finally we see the objects of our craving not as *aśubha* but as being attractive and lovely.

In these verses, Nāgārjuna focuses on that aspect of conditioned existence to which we most easily and regularly ascribe the qualities of loveliness and purity that really belong to the Unconditioned: the body of a person with whom we are infatuated. After all, we don't fall in love with trees, for example, beautiful as they may be. We don't get so attached to a particular tree that we want to spend all our time with it and eventually move in with it. Our craving casts a sort of glamour over the bodies of certain people, a glamour that does not gather around any other object, however beautiful.

Therefore, serious Buddhist practitioners have always been advised to practise the *aśubha bhāvanā*, the contemplation of

83

the less pleasant aspects of the human body. Just as we meditate on the impermanence and insubstantiality of conditioned existence, and on the lack of real satisfaction to be found in it, so we can also meditate on the unattractiveness (*aśubha*) of conditioned existence. In this practice, we focus on certain aspects of the human body, aspects which we would normally find unpleasant but whose unpleasantness we disregard when we are in the grip of sexual passion. The *aśubha bhāvanā* helps to expose how lust can override our natural repugnance for the secretions and excretions of other people's bodies. One tries to see the human body as it really is: impermanent, unsatisfactory, without fixed selfhood, and in truth unlovely.

Buddhist practice involves the cultivation of awareness, but sexual craving, on account of its blind instinctual nature, takes us in the opposite direction. To prevent this from happening, drastic action is needed, and this is what we get in these verses. Nāgārjuna is not necessarily hoping to free the king from sexual desire altogether; he may just be trying to help him to arrive at a degree of awareness. It's as if he is saying, 'Wake up! Take a closer look at this object of your craving. What is it really like?'

His invitation to examine the charms of the flesh with a critical eye perhaps also reflects a thought that at least occasionally crosses the minds of most people when they are engaged in pursuit of someone, or even when they finally achieve an intimate embrace with him or her. Perhaps the first few times you really are exploring the world of pleasurable human experience, but after that you might not be able to help thinking, 'Well, here we go again.' You know more or less what is going to happen, and you wonder, 'Is it really worth doing? What is the point? What am I getting out of this? How much am I even enjoying it?' Yet despite such misgivings, you feel somehow driven to it, as if by compulsion.

In order to counteract such compulsion, there is an emphasis on celibacy in most forms of Buddhism, celibacy being an

84

indication that the sex drive is under control. The Pāli scriptures make it clear that the Buddha was completely celibate, while those who had attained Stream Entry (the point at which progress towards Enlightenment is assured), while not necessarily celibate, were certainly not dominated by their sexual desires. However, in at least one place, the Buddha allows the possibility that someone might enjoy the pleasures of the senses and remain unattached. In the *Ariyapariyesanā Sutta* he classifies practitioners into three types. He uses the image of a deer being hunted, but I'm going to use the image of a mouse as I think this makes the point more clearly. There are three kinds of mice. There are those who go after the cheese in the trap unwisely and who are caught, those who go after the cheese more carefully and who are not caught, and those who stay away from both cheese and trap and who, of course, are not caught. It is interesting that the Buddha did not deny the second possibility, that if you were very mindful you could 'nibble at' the pleasures of the senses without necessarily being overcome by craving. But this is dangerous. Most people are in fact overcome and suffer the consequences. It's much safer to stay away from the cheese. What Nāgārjuna is recommending in the king's case is in principle the second option, which in practice will mean restricting himself to a modest sex life, this being quite compatible with the aim of attaining Stream Entry.

CONTEMPLATION OF BEAUTY

Like celibacy, the *aśubha bhāvanā* is not an end in itself. Disgust or revulsion towards the body cannot be counted as a positive mental state unless it clears the way, as it is meant to do, for something better. In a sense, its purpose is to help us to distinguish between biological attractiveness and aesthetic beauty. One person might have conventional good looks and yet lack any real beauty, while another might be without any obvious attractions, and yet be truly beautiful. *Śubha*, the term used in this context, means pure as well as beautiful. It denotes a kind of spiritual beauty in the Neoplatonic sense. The same kind of beauty is being referred to at the very beginning of the *Precious Garland* when Nāgārjuna extols the Buddha as 'adorned with all good qualities'.

> The Buddha remarks more than once
> in the Pāli scriptures
> that a sign or characteristic of mettā
> is that you see things as beautiful.

The challenge for artists down the centuries has been to paint works that would appeal to their public's taste for sensuous beauty while aiming at the same time to achieve a more innocent vision – an impression of pure beauty – for those who were capable of enjoying it. Even the greatest artists may not always be appreciated for this higher achievement. It is said that at the end of the Second World War, two British soldiers were going round the Uffizi gallery in Florence and came upon Botticelli's 'The Birth of Venus'. 'Oi, come and look at this, Bill', said one, 'There's a girl here with no clothes on and two blokes spitting at her.'

Clearly, beauty isn't necessarily inherent in the object of our perception. It also depends on our looking at it in a certain way. If we look at it with greed or lust, then what we see is something sensuously attractive. If we look at it contemplatively, with *mettā*, then we see something rather different, something possessing beauty. The Buddha remarks more than once in the Pāli scriptures that a sign or characteristic of *mettā* is that you see things as beautiful, *śubha*. This is because the key element in both *śubha* and *mettā*, which raises them above ordinary human emotion, is disinterested awareness.

Schopenhauer emphasized this characteristic of aesthetic appreciation: that it is a pure delight in the object for its own sake, without any desire to make use of it. What he calls the will, 'a striving yearning force', is temporarily suspended. If you find what you see sensuously attractive, you will probably want to grab it for the sake of your own pleasure, but if you find it aesthetically beautiful, you will just want to stand back and contemplate it, surrender to it, absorb yourself in it. Aesthetic contemplation is therefore not only disinterested but in a way impersonal. You lose yourself in the object, forgetting your personal concerns. Thus it is equivalent to the experience of the first *dhyāna*, the first level of meditative absorption.

This is the kind of vision for which the *aśubha bhāvanā* prepares us. Once we have established some initial control over our unskilful reactions to conditioned things, we can begin to reflect on the beauty of the Unconditioned. The *aśubha bhāvanā* helps us to stand back from the object of sensuous desire, to inhibit the impulse to reach out and grasp it, whether literally or mentally. To the extent that we can do this, to that extent we will be able to see things as purely beautiful. Seeing the unloveliness of conditioned existence prepares us to see the beauty that lies beyond it. Conversely, it is difficult to redirect one's desire towards the Unconditioned so long as one imagines that one has found perfect beauty in a particular human form. The positive approach to craving, raising one's gaze from grosser to more refined objects of desire, will be helpful at some point, but a vigorously negative approach is usually necessary to begin with.

Whether everyone could benefit from this approach is another matter. Whereas the Indians of Nāgārjuna's time apparently had a full-blooded and guilt-free relish for worldly pleasures, many in the post-Christian West are still burdened with a vague sense of the sinfulness of sexual pleasure. For us, sex is not quite such a straightforward matter as it seems to have been in ancient India. Someone might therefore take up the *aśubha bhāvanā* with an enthusiasm that came from a rather unhealthy, inhibited, or otherwise negative attitude to their body and their sexuality. In their case, the practice might serve only to reinforce their unhealthy attitude.

I would therefore not prescribe the *aśubha bhāvanā* for very many people in our culture today. Nāgārjuna's advice was offered at a specific time and to a particular person. If he were alive today, he would no doubt express himself in a way that addressed modern problems and preoccupations. For example, he might have thought that a 'romantic' emotional attachment to a particular person in some ways laid deeper snares for the practitioner than sexual desire itself. The processes that underlie such attachments have been investigated by modern psychology. According to Buddhism, we have within us various positive potentials. We are not always conscious of them, however, and we therefore tend to project them – as the psychologists would say – onto objects outside ourselves. We project our spiritual potential, for example, onto a guru figure; and, if we lack confidence, we may project that quality onto someone who appears to possess it. Of course, it is not easy to tell whether one is projecting a positive quality or whether one is simply appreciating its presence in another person in a healthy way. We can be reasonably certain that we will tend to project certain qualities onto those to whom we are sexually attracted. It is as though we were conscious of being somehow incomplete, and that instead of trying to develop what was lacking, we look for it in another person – usually someone of the opposite sex. Married people often refer to their spouse as their 'better half'. This is why people sometimes experience panic and terror when a relationship breaks up. It is as though you were losing far more than just another person; it can feel as though half of you was being torn away. But this is an illusion. The other person is not our other half, as we soon discover if we happen to come into conflict with them. And if a relationship becomes a way of avoiding the task of developing the qualities we believe are possessed by the other person, then it is clearly an unhelpful one.

WORKING WITH
ROMANTIC PROJECTION

Having said all this, projection may be initially useful in that it enables one to have, through contact with another person, some experience of one's unintegrated qualities. In the case of men, it is their unrealized 'feminine' qualities that tend to get projected onto their partner in a romantic relationship – their potential gentleness, sympathy, and receptivity. Because one does not experience certain qualities in oneself, in the sense of not having integrated them into one's conscious being, one is unconsciously drawn to finding them outside oneself.

> As a result of falling out of love
> and possibly breaking up with your partner,
> you will develop, almost naturally,
> a more mature character.

Most people seem to go through this stage of romantic projection, usually in adolescence, and some go on repeating the experience again and again. But if you are relatively healthy, psychologically speaking, and fairly aware, you can learn to withdraw such projections without too much difficulty, and without disrupting your relationship with the other person. All this can be a normal part of growing up. As a result of falling out of love and possibly breaking up with your partner, you will develop, almost naturally, a more mature character.

It is possible to work with our projections even within a close relationship. We just need to ask ourselves, 'What do I really see in this person?' Once we recognize what it is, we know what we need to look for within ourselves. We can also ask ourselves how we feel in the loved person's absence. This is usually a good indication of how far the projection has progressed. When they are not there, do we feel that we ourselves are not really or fully there either, or that we are somehow lost, or helpless? If so, clearly something is missing. It is not

89

just the other person that is missing, but a quality that we have got used to having available to us through them, a quality we experience as being outside rather than within us. Such projection is quite different from appreciating in someone else qualities that we know we ourselves do not possess. We will be pleased to have that person around, and when they are not there we might miss them, but we won't feel that we are being deprived of our very soul.

It is painful when a partner walks out on us, but this is a moment that provides an opportunity to see something about ourselves that perhaps we could not have seen in any other way. Now, at last, we are forced to face the inner lack that this person's presence in our life prevented us from seeing before. Even though we might look around for a substitute to fill the gap, the period of painful awareness into which we have been plunged may enable us to look with more open eyes at the unconscious processes that had been going on.

To conclude, the contemplation of the ugliness of the conditioned needs to be balanced by the contemplation of the purely beautiful. We need the stick *and* the carrot. I would suggest only that the carrot should be carefully chosen. In some circles it seems to be regarded as old-fashioned to look for beauty in the arts, but perhaps this is due to a confusion between true beauty and the merely pretty and decorative. Though one might react against the Victorian weakness for the picturesque and the sentimental, this is not a reason for turning one's back on what is truly beautiful, whether in art or in nature.

Many years ago I got to know a film producer in Bombay who, despite his busy and glamorous life, was quite thoughtful. He once visited the Ajanta caves to look for a film location, and on his return he had a question for me. He had been impressed, he said, by the beauty of the cave paintings, but one thing puzzled him. He had noticed there were not only paintings of Buddhas and Bodhisattvas, and of animals and plants, but also of half-naked women. Why, he asked, had the monks who lived there, whose lives were dedicated to the practice of renunciation, depicted such images on the walls of their dwelling? I had not considered this question before, but the answer that immediately came to me was that the monks must have regarded the bodies of women as being simply part of the natural world, and that they were, as such, to be appreciated like other beautiful objects. They saw them aesthetically, not with desire, just as they saw fruit and flowers. One Buddhist approach is to reject these objects of craving altogether, and to persuade oneself that they aren't really quite so attractive after all. But perhaps aesthetic appreciation provides a middle way between complete rejection of craving and complete abandonment of oneself to it. This, it seems to me, is the ideal solution to the problem of sexual craving, and one that is well within the capacity of the serious Buddhist.

The implication here is that we need to derive pleasure from life, even – indeed especially – from a life of renunciation. There is not much point in steering clear of sexual involvements if you are unable to find pleasure anywhere else. If you find your spiritual practice a difficult, painful struggle, and your only enjoyments are crude, sensual ones, you have a problem. A simple solution is to find enjoyment in meditation. Don't take pride in undertaking marathon sessions for their own sake. A twenty-minute meditation that you enjoy is better than an hour's meditation that you do only because it is supposed to be good for you. Look for a natural momentum to take you deeper, beyond the imposed discipline that may have been necessary at the beginning. Broaden the scope of your interests to include innocent recreations that you can share with friends, especially spiritual friends. Let at least some of the skilful things you do be enjoyable. A Buddhist should be a walking paradox in the eyes of the world: he or she should be obviously happy, even in the absence of financial security, social status, luxury consumer goods, or a sexual relationship – all of which are commonly regarded as being essential to human happiness. The sight of such a person would make people wonder, 'How can this be? Perhaps my ideas about life are not the whole story.' It is what a Buddhist *is* that speaks to people, far more than clever presentations of Buddhist doctrine. It is where you look for your happiness and satisfaction, much more than what you talk about, that tells people who you really are and what you stand for.

Try bringing an aesthetically appreciative, rather than a utilitarian, attitude to your experience. Obviously we shouldn't just make use of others. We should try to shake off the attitude that sees attractive people, for example, as being simply objects of desire, underlying which is a view of people and the world around us as having value only as they contribute to our own enjoyment or advantage. The aesthetic attitude is one that sees everything, including other people, with a warm and clear awareness, and appreciates things just as they are, without thinking how they could be improved or put to some use. It is akin to the contemplative attitude of resting in pure awareness, without experiencing either desire or aversion. This certainly requires mindfulness, but it is a practice that will reduce the pressure of craving, and leave you feeling more at ease.

4

SKILFUL SPEECH

Refraining completely from false,
Divisive, harsh, and senseless speech[35]

Abstention from false speech is the only speech precept in the traditional list of five precepts, the *pañcaśīla*. In the list of ten precepts, however, one of the *pañcaśīla* – abstaining from intoxicants – is left out, and replaced with three further speech precepts and three 'mind-training' precepts whose practice requires an additional level of awareness. These are ethical guidelines for Buddhists who wish to undertake a serious, 'full-time' practice of the Dharma. The emphasis on speech is very significant. In the West, the traditional division of our nature is mind and body, or body, soul, and spirit. In Buddhism the division is into body, speech, and mind, according to which analysis our capacity to communicate ourselves is accorded an equal place with our physical being and our inner experience.

As Buddhists, when we bow before a Buddha image, we do so by joining our hands and touching our forehead, throat, and chest in succession, in this way connecting with the psycho-physical energy centres or chakras at those points which, according to the Tantric tradition, are associated with, respectively, body, speech, and mind. In doing this, we are symbolically offering the whole of ourselves to the ideal of Enlightenment, as represented by the Buddha, without holding anything back. Speech brings together head and heart, intellect and emotion, body and mind, and, of course, self and other.

The speech precepts are not just about being truthful. One's speech should also be kindly and helpful and it should bring about harmony rather than being harsh, senseless, or divisive. These four speech precepts reflect four progressive levels of human communication. First, there is the level of simple truthfulness, of abstention from false speech, *musāvādā*. Next, there is the level of kindly or affectionate speech, of abstention from harsh speech, *pharusavācā*. This involves being aware to whom one is speaking and being aware of their response. It should, after all, be possible to express oneself freely and cogently while at the same time considering the feelings of whoever one is addressing.

As a baby, one knows one's mother only as a wonderful sensation of warmth and comfort, security and well-being; one is not aware of her as a person. When grown up, one often knows people in much the same way, but refined and rationalized. This is one of the reasons why there are so many misunderstandings between people. Much 'communication' is pseudo-communication – communication between mutual projections. But speaking with affection is an attempt to communicate with a genuine awareness of the other person, quite apart from what they might be able to do for one physically, materially, or emotionally. Abstaining from harsh speech in the course of a debate requires extra mindfulness because it is very easy to get carried away, especially if one is very articulate. Some people get more and more heated about increasingly remote aspects of the original issue, until, in the end, they are just sounding off, having entirely lost sight of the existence of the other participants and forgotten the context of the discussion.

The third level of communication is that of meaningful and helpful speech, which is the positive counterpart of the precept of abstention from senseless speech, *samphappalāpavācā*. Most people think that senseless or frivolous speech is relatively harmless. Those with no desire to become more aware will probably be quite happy talking trivialities for the rest of their lives. If you become more mindful, though, you will notice that while a little small talk oils the wheels of communication, a whole session of it can be quite draining. This is because, while part of you is caught up in the banter, the more serious part of you is frustrated. You feel that you have betrayed your better self, and the resulting sense of conflict will be draining. This is not to say that you need to be talking about the Dharma morning, noon, and night, but that at the very least, you should abstain from spending too much time on small talk. Aim to make sure that whatever you say is meaningful and helpful.

The fourth level of communication is that of bringing about harmony between people, the positive counterpart of abstention from divisive speech, known as *pisuṇavācā*. This does not mean avoiding disagreement at all costs. It means speech that transcends selfhood, speech that leaves behind self-interest and helps to bring about a happier and more peaceful community. Between two or more people, the harmonious communication may culminate, eventually, in silence – a rich and living silence in which there is a common experience of self-transcendence. To develop this level of communication one can begin by cultivating an awareness of a deeper and more authentic level of being in the other person, particularly in a spiritual friend, and most importantly in one's spiritual teacher. Try to contact the real person behind the physical form, behind the words, and relate to what is deepest – or highest – in them. The fullest experience of harmonious speech takes place only between Enlightened human beings, between whom there is no barrier of selfhood.

THE PATH OF TRUTH

Just as by themselves the true words
Of kings generate firm trust,
So their false words are the best means
To create distrust.

What is not deceitful is the truth;
It is not an intentional fabrication.
What is solely helpful to others is the truth.
The opposite is falsehood since it does not help.[36]

Ideally, a democratic government would tell the electorate the truth, but there are a number of reasons why this does not always happen. First of all, in a complex political or economic situation the truth is rarely obvious. Even if all the facts are known, they do not necessarily tell you what is really going on. What you take to be the truth of the matter will differ from what others take to be the truth, and you will need to bear in mind the limitations of your own point of view.

> The spiritual life is a matter of seeking the truth
> and learning to live by it, whatever the cost.

Secondly, people do not necessarily want to be told the truth, and politicians often have to tell the public what it likes to hear in order to win popularity. For example, people prefer a politician who claims to be in control of events rather than one who admits to being at a loss – which is perhaps understandable.

Thirdly, in a democracy politicians band together to win elections and then stay in power. They therefore have to put their party first, sometimes at the expense of their own conscience.

They are obliged to toe the party line, to subordinate their own view of the truth of a situation to the collective interest of the party to which they belong. What politicians probably tell themselves is that paltering with the truth is the price that has to be paid if they are to do all the good things they have promised to do in their manifesto. It is a grubby expedience for the sake of achieving worthy ends.

But such rationalizations are not convincing. The first aim of a politician should be to deserve people's trust, for once trust has been lost it is irretrievable. What the public does not realize is that it asks, in effect, for untrustworthy politicians. It votes for people who are plausible, and who will tell it reassuring untruths. It is only when there is a crisis that the general public insists on knowing the truth, and by then it is often too late. If you begin by telling the truth and go on telling it, you might have to spend a long time in the wilderness and not be believed in your own lifetime. But at least people will trust you to speak the truth as you see it, however unpalatable they might find it.

The choice between truth and reassurance is often a hard one to make, but it is one that the spiritual life, at bottom, is all about. The spiritual life is a matter of seeking the truth and learning to live by it, whatever the cost. It is much easier to criticize others, especially politicians, than it is to conduct our own affairs in accordance with our professed Buddhist values. Speaking the truth begins at home. As Buddhists, our first duty, in our capacity as citizens, is to be straightforward and honest in all our dealings. Preaching comes a long way after that.

In saying that the truth is that which is helpful, Nāgārjuna is suggesting that truth is something more than simple facts. Truth is not a thing to be dumped on people. It is a truthful *communication*. Truth is non-deception in action. Facts can be known in a coldly objective way, but knowing the truth involves appreciating what those facts mean for people, and how

97

they connect with them. The time has to be right, the other person has to be receptive, and we ourselves have to be in a positive, kindly frame of mind. If the other person misunderstands what we have said or takes unreasonable offence, then we cannot really be said to have 'spoken the truth' in the full sense.

But even when speaking the truth causes pain, we have at some point to work our way round to it. We cannot indefinitely put off the day we actually speak the truth, the day we say what we really think. Let us be gentle and sensitive, certainly, and tactful if we can be so, but in the long run it is only the truth that is going to help people, not a pleasant falsehood.

The way to cultivate truthful speech varies from one person to another. The person who is liable to blurt out the truth without thinking, who talks first and thinks later, will have to learn to turn things over in their mind, while someone who is inhibited and tends to keep things back will need to be less fearful, less self-censoring.

> In the end, you can speak the truth in abstract conceptual terms only to someone who knows it already – which means that it is not really a communication.

The idea that speech should be helpful implies that truth may be subordinate to the principle of 'skilful means'. The classic example of this is the parable of the burning house in the *Lotus Sūtra*. A father wants to get all his numerous children out of the house when it is engulfed by flames, so he tells them he has various toy carts for them, and that these are waiting outside. The children run out of the house in wild excitement to find they have been deceived. The carts they hoped for are not there. But their father goes on to give each of them a far bigger and better cart than they could have imagined in their wildest dreams. The father represents the Buddha, of course, and the burning house represents *saṃsāra*, the world wherein human beings are engrossed in their various 'games'. The question is, how far should we take this story as a model for the communication of the Dharma?

First of all, the story should not be taken literally. It is a parable. It is not an account of how a teacher gets people practising the Dharma by telling them tall stories; it is about a father doing whatever was necessary in a life-or-death situation. We should be careful to be as open and direct as we can in our communication of the Dharma and not induce people to practise it by promising them worldly benefits of one kind or another as a result of their efforts. Even if they are expected subsequently to discover for themselves the limitations of those benefits as compared with the spiritual rewards of practising the Dharma, the fact is that they will have been deceived. The deception does not relate to the material benefits, which may well follow, but concerns the nature of the transformation brought about by the practice of the Dharma, which is essentially a transformation of the mind, not one's material fortunes. Though we may indeed gain a measure of worldly happiness through our practice of the Dharma, that happiness should be less important to us than growth in our understanding of the Dharma.

Thus the parable of the burning house needs to be interpreted carefully. Higher spiritual experience is always going to be more than we can anticipate theoretically. It will always exceed our expectations. Reality is always infinitely greater than any description of it, and any description will, to that extent, be misleading. When you attain *nirvāṇa*, is it going to be what you thought it would be? Of course not. But has the Buddha deceived you? No. It is just that you needed to be told something about it, even if what you were told was so utterly inadequate to the reality as to be, from the point of view of *nirvāṇa* itself, a complete misrepresentation. When the father promises toys to his children, he is being as truthful as he can. One

99

could say that the cart he finally gives each of them is the same as the little carts he promised, but on an infinitely grander scale.

Much the same thing happens in the course of ordinary life. When you grow up, when you marry and have a child, are these events anything like what you originally envisaged? Almost certainly not. The same goes for when you receive Buddhist ordination, or when you yourself ordain someone. But were you deceived when you were told what to expect? No. All these events represent a breakthrough that could not be understood in terms of any previous experience. On its own much higher level, *nirvāṇa* resembles such break-throughs. In the end, you can speak the truth in abstract conceptual terms only to someone who knows it already – which means that it is not really a communication. We might therefore say that the truth is that which produces positive results, or which leads one in a positive direction.

Returning to the first of the four speech precepts, abstention from false speech, we may say that it requires, as do the other precepts, that we pay attention to the subtle ways in which we evade their spirit. For example, we sometimes confuse objective facts with our subjective interpretation of those facts without being aware that in so doing we are misrepresenting them. Underlying this tendency is the assumption that our view of things is the correct one, an assumption that simply reinforces our confusion. If we are unable to accept that our perceptions are conditioned by our confused views and by our assumptions generally, we preclude the possibility of our ever changing our view.

> We must be careful not to evaluate
> when we should be simply describing.

False speech often hides behind jargon. Instead of saying, for example, 'He's not being open with me,' or 'I'm afraid she isn't very receptive,' it might be more honest for one to say, 'He (or she) does not agree with me.' A failure to accept one's point of view *might* be because of a lack of openness or receptivity, but on the other hand it might be due to a genuine disagreement, to the fact that the other person thinks differently. We must be careful not to evaluate when we should simply be describing. To assert that somebody is not being open can be a dishonest way of winning the argument and shows a lack of understanding of what openness really means. Being open does not necessarily mean agreeing. Someone can be very receptive to what you say and sincerely try to understand your point of view but, in the end, disagree with you. Conversely, someone might not really be open to you at all, but might agree with you out of politeness.

Obviously you want the other person to agree with you, but if they refuse to do so, it simply means that you have been unable to convince them. To misrepresent them by saying – to take another example – 'I got a very negative response,' amounts to false speech. Did the other person fly into a temper and hit you over the head with a chair, or did they simply disagree with you? The danger of using psycho-spiritual jargon, like 'openness', 'receptivity', 'commitment', is that while our intention may be to use it to evaluate our mental states and cultivate positive ones, it can also be used in such a way as to put in the wrong someone who really does aspire to be open, receptive, and so on. As well as manipulating language, such jargon manipulates other people. It can be a kind of emotional blackmail, as if one was to say, 'You want to be committed, open, and receptive. So why not agree with me?' Such jargon represents an extra layer of false speech for us to deal with. When someone says, 'I'm sorry, I can't help you on this occasion,' do you find yourself saying they are unwilling to cooperate? Or do you report what they actually said, even though you might feel disappointed with their attitude and suspect they are being deliberately uncooperative?

Other examples of psycho-spiritual jargon include 'rationalization' and 'projection'. We know that these complex self-deluding processes do take place, and that they sometimes need to be taken into consideration, and this is what gives words of this kind their edge when they are used in an accusatory manner. The golden rule is to point out the possibly unconscious basis of what another person says or does only privately and tentatively. Say, 'It may be my imagination, and I may be completely wrong, but this is what I think. At least give it some thought.' Motives can indeed be questioned, but one should not try to rebut someone's argument simply by questioning their motives, and certainly not by questioning allegedly unconscious ones. If someone disagrees with you, it does not necessarily mean that there is something psychologically wrong with them.

At the root of the whole issue is the insistence that one's feelings about something should be accorded the kind of objective validity that one would not claim for one's thinking. Rather than say 'I think' or 'this is my impression', one says, 'I feel'. Someone might say, 'I feel that so-and-so is not very committed to the Dharma,' and another person might point out that he meditates for three hours a day, lives in a single-sex Buddhist community, works in a team-based right livelihood business, studies the Dharma regularly, and helps out around the local Buddhist centre. But then the first person looks very thoughtful and replies, 'That's true, but still my *feeling* is that he's not very committed.' Apparently, one is expected to give to that feeling the status of an objective, evidential fact about the person being discussed.

The confusion arises when it is assumed that another person's feelings cannot be questioned, because they are, *ipso facto*, only verifiable by them, whereas rational arguments can be challenged by anyone. If for an argument you substitute a feeling – especially an *intuitive* feeling – you thereby preclude the possibility of any rational discussion. For example, if you feel that someone's attitude towards you is very negative, the next question to arise is often not 'Where does this feeling of mine come from?' but 'Why does he have a negative attitude towards me?' If you go ahead and ask, 'Why do you have a negative attitude towards me?' and the poor fellow replies, 'Actually, I don't feel negative towards you,' you can then point out, helpfully, 'Your trouble is that you're not really in touch with your feelings.'

Arguing in an emotional way can be a variation on this kind of obfuscation of the truth. It usually has the virtue of being artless, though there is a classic example that is by no means artless: that of the clergyman who wrote in the margin of his sermon, 'Shout here – argument weak.' The emotional emphasis with which a person says something tells us nothing about the truth of that statement. It tells us only about the strength of the conviction with which it was made.

All this is part of the larger issue of false speech by default or *suppressio veri, suggestio falsi*: suppression of the truth, suggestion of falsehood. It might be appropriate to speculate about someone's motives, but subjective views should not be confused with objective facts. If you don't know the reason for someone's absence from an important meeting, for example, it would be false speech to remark, 'So-and-so is failing in his commitment tonight.' Underneath the layer of assumptions there will always be a layer of fact, and that layer of fact is what you must get down to, however uncertain it might leave you as to how to judge a person or a situation.

THE CONSEQUENCES OF UNSKILFUL SPEECH

From lying arises slander.
From divisiveness, a parting of friends.
From harshness, hearing the unpleasant.
From senselessness, one's speech is not respected.[37]

Speech is the area of activity in which much of our ethical practice takes place. It is the first – and often the only – outlet through which our thoughts and feelings find expression. Nāgārjuna's theme here is that when we speak unskilfully we do not, in fact, get what we hoped for. He is pointing out that when we try to secure some kind of advantage at someone else's expense by telling lies, we get a poor return. The more calculating we are, the more we find that our sums just don't add up. So why then do we lie, for example? Lying often seems to be an easy way of getting the better of someone. But Nāgārjuna reminds us that the advantage will be short-lived. If we tell lies, we are relying on people taking our given word for the truth, and that kind of trust is a priceless asset. But sooner or later we will be found out, and our word will then be worth nothing, at least in some quarters. Moreover, telling lies creates an atmosphere of mistrust in which others may be afraid to speak the truth. When lies become the accepted currency of communication, truth becomes worthless. If, for example, we pass the blame for something we have done onto someone else, that person might feel they have the right to do the same in their turn. It is likely, therefore, that at some point we will be made to bear the blame for someone else's misdeeds. We don't have to wait for another life in order to experience the consequences of our own unskilful speech.

The same goes for the other forms of unskilful speech. They, too, seem to produce consequences (*karma vipāka*) quite promptly. By divisive speech is meant tittle-tattle, backbiting, malicious gossip, creating dissension and disharmony between people: basically, causing your friends and acquaintances to think worse of one another than they did before you opened your mouth. Maybe you repeat to one person what another person said about them, or you tell someone an amusing story that reveals something discreditable about a friend of theirs. In this way, you undermine trust and respect between people, and the result is that the dissension and disharmony you have created eventually engulfs you.

If we have a criticism to make about someone, it is far better to make it to them directly. If we criticize others behind their backs, we might be surprised to find how often our criticism reaches the person criticized. We might not hear anything about the matter for a long time, but we can never be sure that we won't, and one day we might get a nasty shock, especially if the person in question turns out to have a perfectly good explanation for the conduct with which we have found fault. This can happen quite easily between friends, if they have the kind of relationship that skirts around difficult issues. If they air those issues with other people instead of the person concerned, the result is likely to be a falling out and even a parting.

In the case of harsh speech we often find our unskilfulness reflected back to us quite quickly. Its painful effect is felt immediately and we can therefore expect a swift reaction. We will at least create around us an unpleasant atmosphere, one that may even flare up into violence and that will not easily be calmed down. If we engage in harsh speech, it is as though we expect others to bear it patiently, and they will not always do this. People might do our bidding when we speak harshly, but they will give us a wide berth if they can.

> Ideally, even in the case of an old friend, we should feel that we do not really know who we are now meeting.

The result of idle and useless talk is that what we say is not respected. If someone is in the habit of talking nonsense, perhaps to entertain or just to be noticed, in the end no one will take them seriously. Consequently, when they do talk seriously, they may not get the kind of attention they want. Other people will think, 'It's only so-and-so babbling away as usual', and turn a deaf ear. But we should, in fact, make a point of trying to take seriously even people who are in the habit of talking frivolously. We don't know whether someone is chattering foolishly to avoid meaningful talk or to compensate for not being listened to in the first place. Moreover, a licensed fool is rarely a complete fool, and like King Lear's fool, they might have things to say that no one else is prepared to point out.

One of the results of breaking precepts, particularly ones we break frequently, like the speech precepts, is that people start giving us labels. Acquiring labels and labelling others can be useful from a practical point of view. If someone is habitually late for appointments, or is forgetful, or indeed is punctual or conscientious, it is useful to know this. But we have to be careful with labels, especially negative ones. Once they are applied they can be difficult to remove, even when they are no longer appropriate, as in the case of someone who turns over a new leaf. Labels should be provisional, and it is important both to challenge the labels we ourselves are given and to question those we bestow on others. Otherwise we are likely to have a closed attitude to the people we meet, and thus to block both our own development and theirs. Parents are particularly prone to see their grown-up offspring in this fixed way, wanting to see them just as they were when young. As a result, the offspring can find themselves reverting to their teenage selves whenever they go home on a visit.

But we all have a tendency to burden others with our judgements, even to the extent of labelling them for life. Our fixed view of ourselves and of the world is based largely on our habit of stereotyping. For example, if someone is known for their rough tongue and bad temper, even if they are making a determined effort to be patient, we may not let go of our view of them. 'Maybe he's not showing it,' we might concede, sceptically, 'but he's clearly still very angry underneath.' If someone's efforts to change are not appreciated because of such cynicism, they might decide that it isn't worth trying, and revert to type. The same goes for the idle chatterer, or someone seen as lazy or irresponsible. Once they have a label, they may be stuck with it for life, unless they move somewhere else and make a fresh start. However, once you are determined to change, some labels can quite easily be removed. If you have a reputation for meanness, say, you can quite easily change people's perception of you by being so generous that they are sure to notice. If you tend to be late you can make a point of always being punctual, and people will get the message sooner or later. Some labels of course are much harder to remove.

One of the functions of the spiritual community is to encourage people to change. That is, we should try to see other people as individuals. An individual, a true individual, cannot easily be labelled or categorized. Ultimately, such an individual becomes free of labels altogether: people may try to label him or her, but their labels will not stick. This possibility has to be nurtured by a culture that does not feed our human tendency to label people. When we meet them, especially members of the spiritual community, it should be as though we met them for the first time, rather than seeing them on the basis of how we saw them in the past. Usually we don't know what conditions brought about our impressions of them, whether our own prejudices or the context in which we first met them. If we have only met them once before, we might have caught them at an uncharacteristic moment. Ideally, even in the case of an old friend, we should feel that we do not really know who we are now meeting. That attitude of openness in itself can make it possible for them to change.

HEARING THE TRUTH

Wisdom and practice always grow
For one who keeps company
With those who speak advisedly,
Who are pure, and who have unstained wisdom and compassion.

Rare are helpful speakers,
Listeners are very rare,
But rarer still are those who act at once
On words that though unpleasant are beneficial.

Therefore having realized that though unpleasant
It is helpful, act on it quickly,
Just as to cure an illness one drinks
Dreadful medicine from one who cares.[38]

Truth is relational: it depends partly (although only partly) upon who is hearing it. It follows that being able to hear the truth is just as important as being able to tell it. In a sense, they are different aspects of the same ethical practice. Nāgārjuna points out that people who can listen to beneficial speech are rarer than those who are able to speak it. This is obvious, really, because it is easier to see the truth about other people than it is to see the truth about oneself, even if another is very ready to tell us about it. We tend to resist the truth about ourselves, even pleasant truth sometimes. As for helpful but unpleasant 'home truths', it is certainly easier for most people to give someone else such bitter medicine than to swallow it themselves.

> If you have, or can develop,
> the ability to hear truths that are difficult to accept,
> this is a great quality.

If an attempt to communicate was not a success and we find ourselves saying, 'I was only trying to be helpful,' it may be that the other person was not receptive, but alternatively it may be that we simply misunderstood them. It is difficult both to see the truth about someone and to communicate it to them in such a way that they can receive it. Above all, we need to be sure that we have their true welfare at heart, and that we are not simply speaking out of frustration or irritation. We can easily deceive ourselves in this regard. It is important that we communicate love and kindness, and affectionate concern for the other person's well-being, as well as communicating the helpful truth.

If you have, or can develop, the ability to hear truths that are difficult to accept, this is a great quality, especially in a leader. If you are able to put aside your immediate emotional reactions and rationalizations, you should take the medicine quickly – that is, accept the unpleasant truth and act upon it at once. It is easier to respond positively when you have known the person giving you the unwelcome information for some time. When they have demonstrated their affection for you time and time again over a number of years, you know that they can be trusted to have your welfare at heart, even if they speak rather bluntly.

5

THE ETHICS OF VIEWS

Thoroughly forsaking covetousness, harmful intent,
And the views of Nihilists –[39]

This is Nāgārjuna's succinct reference to the three 'mind precepts': undertaking to abstain from covetousness, animosity,
and false views. Covetousness and animosity in their various
forms are discussed in the next chapter, so here we will concentrate for the most part on what it means to abstain from
false views.

ETERNALISM AND NIHILISM

It might seem that 'the views of Nihilists' belong to a completely different category of mental experience from covetousness and harmful intent, but for Buddhism there is a
crucial connection between emotions and views, between
negative emotions and spiritual ignorance. We feel the way we
do because of the way we see things, and we see things the way
we do because of the way we feel about them. Nihilism, for

example, is ultimately connected with hatred, while its opposite, eternalism, is connected with craving.

Nihilism translates the Sanskrit term *ucchedavāda*, which literally means the 'ism' of 'cutting off'. This is the view that at death one is cut off completely, that there is no psychic or mental element that survives the dissolution of the body. One could call it annihilationism. The opposite view, that of eternalism, maintains that one possesses an unchanging psychic essence, a permanent self or soul that exists independently of the body and continues to exist after death. Buddhism does not take either of these positions, but understands consciousness to be a stream, a flow of ever-changing mental events that continues from life to life, linking with one body after another, though not as a *thing* or entity that could be said to transmigrate or reincarnate. This is why Buddhism speaks of 'rebirth' or 'rebecoming' rather than of 'reincarnation'.

These two views seem to be intrinsic to the way the unenlightened mind sees things. Take, for example, *nirvāṇa*, the ultimate goal of the Buddhist spiritual life. Because the term literally means 'blowing out (as of a flame)', it is easy to take a nihilistic view of it, to think of it as a 'state' of non-existence into which one disappears upon gaining Enlightenment. On the other hand, if *nirvāṇa* is thought of as a kind of heaven in which one continues to exist after achieving Enlightenment, albeit in a subtle and sublimated form, one is labouring under a delusion of the eternalist kind. The truth is that Enlightenment transcends both these views. It is indescribable in terms of being or non-being, existence or non-existence, life or death. It is unclassifiable, belonging to no category of thought whatsoever. One can say neither that the self is annihilated, nor that it continues to exist. *Nirvāṇa* does not exist as we understand existence; neither does it not exist; nor is it anything in between.

An ancient eternalist wrong view, put forward in the Buddha's day by a teacher called Makkhali Gosāla, is that there are just 1,406,600 different kinds of life to be lived, and that after passing through all of these and thus exhausting all the possibilities of existence, one automatically attains *nirvāṇa*.[40] Certain 'New Age' views are similar to this. One is here on Earth to learn certain lessons from one's present existence before progressing to the next life and the next lesson. There is also the view that the 'Age of Aquarius', a sort of collective raising of human consciousness, is upon us. According to this view, we are to be carried away by a great wave of spiritual regeneration into the 'New Age', whether we like it or not. The general idea is that spiritual evolution happens automatically, and that it is, in fact, inevitable.

The mistake that is common to these wrong views is their conflating of biological evolution and spiritual development. They all leave out the crucial element of individual decision. The increasingly complex development of life-forms over millions of years has brought us a long way, from single-celled amoeba right up to the human organism, but from now on, our development depends upon our own initiative, our own individual effort. If we sit back and wait for the Age of Aquarius to dawn, we shall have to wait a very long time. Buddhism itself may seem to promote this kind of eternalistic wrong view in its doctrine of the Pure Land (see page 179). However, the Pure Land comes into being as the result of a Bodhisattva's determination to help 'the infinite number of beings inhabiting limitless space' by creating for them a situation in which the Dharma is more easily *practised*. There is never going to be a kind of spiritual welfare state. The goal for everyone is to be oneself a creator of a Pure Land, not an endless consumer of spiritual goodies.

> The middle way is to appreciate life as much as we can
> but not hang on to it,
> and to appreciate death when it comes
> but neither long for it nor fear it.

Of these two evasions of reality, the Buddha singled out nihilism as representing the worst tendencies of spiritual ignorance. He was of the view that if you *had* to choose between eternalism, the belief that things have an unchanging essence, and nihilism, the belief that there is no such thing as karma and that death means extinction, eternalism would be the better option.[41] Eternalists at least have an affirmative attitude to life. They believe in something positive. For example, the eternalist view that there is an afterlife that lasts for ever may be unfounded, but it does at least provide a basis for consistent and constructive courses of action aimed at definite goals, besides instilling a sense of responsibility towards other people.

Nihilism runs very deep, and it is the underlying source of innumerable superficially plausible wrong views. The way in which one sees through it will depend upon what sort of nihilist you are, and how the nihilism has managed to get so firmly rooted in your mind. According to the Pāli scriptures, the Buddha linked eternalism with craving for existence and nihilism with craving for non-existence, or the longing for oblivion. The eternalist position seems natural enough: if you are an eternalist your attachment to your own being is such that you will see yourself as continuing to exist after Enlightenment, more or less unchanged, but free from suffering. But what causes a person to crave for non-existence? The Buddha seems to have seen nihilism as a rationalization of self-hatred. Perhaps fearing what might happen after death, perhaps on 'Judgement Day', you prefer to live your life in the belief that it is all going to come to a full stop, that you won't have to put up with yourself for ever. Alternatively, it may be that you are simply weary of life and would not willingly undergo more of it under the painful terms that appear to be the only ones on offer. It may seem that existence consists of nothing but suffering and that there is no positive exit. Unfortunately, a negative experience of life tends to translate into a negative view of death and of anything that might come after it. If all you can imagine is a great reckoning and (perhaps literally)

hell to pay in the next life, or more of the same dreadful experience that you have had already, you may well be drawn to
embrace the idea that there is nothing after death. According
to Buddhism, belief in nihilism leads to an unhappy rebirth,
and it would certainly seem that a consciousness imbued with
despair and a loathing for life would have this kind of result.

However, even if you do have a generally unhappy experience
of life, there is no need to make it the basis for the kind of
nihilistic outlook that will have a bad outcome in terms of
karma vipāka. It is possible to separate a painful experience
from an unskilful reaction. Indeed, much Buddhist practice
consists in doing just this. For example, why should you not,
instead, view death as a great 'wiping the slate clean' in which
you can forget everything and start afresh? It may be that in
the experience of death you will be able to forget the
sufferings of your previous existence, in which case your natural desire for life and its enjoyments should emerge once
more. On the strength of this great forgetting you will be able
to start all over again. Previous lives, after all, must have
brought you a fair share of suffering, but how much of it have
you remembered? For most people, even the suffering
endured long ago in their present life eventually loses its sting.
Many things that seemed desperately important at the time
are virtually forgotten in a few months or years, and surely this
will be even more so in the case of a future existence. We will
carry into it our karmic propensities, but not the circumstances in which they were originally formed.

These matters of life and death are not easy for any of us to
deal with, regardless of whether we are eternalist or nihilist by
temperament or by conviction. But we need to find a middle
way, and here, the middle way is to appreciate life as much as
we can but not hang on to it, and to appreciate death when it
comes but neither long for it nor fear it.

THE EMPTINESS OF THE CONDITIONED

In brief the view of nihilism
Is that effects of actions do not exist.
Without merit and leading to a bad state,
It is regarded as a 'wrong view'.

In brief the view of existence
Is that effects of actions exist.
Meritorious and conducive to happy transmigrations
It is regarded as a 'right view'.

Because existence and non-existence are extinguished by wisdom,
There is a passage beyond meritorious and ill deeds.
This, say the excellent, is liberation from
Bad transmigrations and happy transmigrations.[42]

Nihilism is the view that after death nothing of you remains, that the mind perishes with the body, that there is no rebirth, and that there is, therefore, no future karmic fruit of one's actions committed in the present life. This is of course a prevalent modern view, even among those who call themselves Buddhists. Nāgārjuna says here that wrong view, in this case nihilism, leads to low status, whereas right view, which as described here is a form of eternalism, which may include an eternalist view of *nirvāṇa*, leads to high status. If you hold such an eternalist view, you are at least on the right track to an extent. But any position within the wheel of becoming – depicted symbolically by the Tibetan Wheel of Life – falls short of Enlightenment. *Nirvāṇa* is beyond both low and high status. It is freedom from the whole cycle, liberation from 'good' as well as 'bad' rebirth. So long as you remain within the wheel of becoming, you are a prisoner. Simply to be reclassified as a prisoner with special privileges is no answer to your basic problem. Right view leads to good rebirths; wrong view leads to bad rebirths; 'no view' leads to *nirvāṇa*.

Wisdom is a dynamic understanding of experience that sees things as process or flux. It is this wisdom that destroys the static view of 'is' and 'is not', and that provides us with a way beyond the ups as well as the downs of the wheel of becoming, beyond high status as well as low status.

Seeing production as caused
One passes beyond non-existence,
Seeing cessation as caused
One also does not assert existence.[43]

This is the basic Buddhist view that the things we experience in ourselves and the world around us exist in dependence upon conditions and cease when those conditions cease. The nature of the conditioned mind is such that we treat things as though they were absolutely real when in fact they consist in a temporary coming together of factors, both objective and sub-jective, that are themselves conditioned by other factors.

Seeing the coming into being of conditioned things, one is aware that they are produced by causes or conditions. In doing so, one sees through the nihilistic view that they arise without cause – that is, 'one passes beyond non-existence'. Seeing also the cessation of conditioned things, and understanding that this too is the product of causes or conditions, one no longer asserts their prior existence independent of causes.

Previously produced and simultaneously produced (causes)
Are non-causes; (thus) there are no causes in fact,
Because (such) production is not confirmed at all
As (existing) conventionally or in reality.

When this is, that arises,
Like short when there is long.
Due to the production of this, that is produced,
Like light from the production of a flame.

When there is long, there is short.
They do not exist through their own nature,
Just as due to the non-production
Of a flame, light also does not arise.

Having thus seen that effects arise
From causes, one asserts what appears
In the conventions of the world
And does not accept nihilism.

One who asserts, just as it is, cessation
That does not arise from conventions
Does not pass into (a view of) existence.
Thereby one not relying on duality is liberated.[44]

So here, while we are still in the realm of ethical practice, we are plunged deeper and deeper into the 'Perfection of Wisdom' of which Nāgārjuna was such a master. Here he is saying that if a cause appears before the effect, it cannot be a cause in itself – it becomes a cause only with the arrival of the effect. If, on the other hand, cause and effect arise at one and the same time, their relationship cannot be causal, because by definition causes must precede effects. A cause is essentially an idea, a way of connecting up what we insist on seeing as separate items and entities. The idea of a cause is dependent on the idea of an effect. A cause cannot exist as a cause before the effect that has made it a cause has itself come into existence. If the cause exists before the effect has come into existence, it is not yet a cause, only something that happens. On the other hand, when the effect has happened, the 'cause' cannot be a cause either. The effect has already taken place, so does not need a cause to bring it into being.

To deny the existence of a 'self'
while offering a world of self-existent entities
is simply alienating, without that denial having any effect
upon the deep-seated delusion of selfhood.

117

In other words, once you start thinking of cause and effect as entities having real existence, you find yourself involved in all sorts of logical contradictions. But this is more than just a clever trick of logic. It repays serious reflection. Our ideas of cause and effect subtly determine the way in which we interpret experience even while we are experiencing it. The relations between things, and even the things themselves, are not by any means always what we assume them to be. By understanding cause as cause only in relation to effect, we start seeing through the view of things as entities having real existence and consequently become less attached to them. In this way we gradually let go of 'a view of existence', that is, the idea of something or someone actually existing. In terms of ultimate reality, there is not even any coming into being or any ceasing to be. These ideas also are the result of limited ways of thinking. There is not some pre-existing 'thing' that is produced, nor any 'thing' that ceases to exist. Nāgārjuna rejects that entire static and rigid way of thinking, turning it upon itself to expose its invalidity.

In getting rid of the idea of a world of fixed entities, we enlist the help of the ideas of process, conditionality, even cause and effect. If, however, we come to regard these ideas as representing actual entities, we are simply repeating the same mistake on another level. Nāgārjuna is saying that cause and effect are relative terms: you cannot think of cause without effect, or effect without cause, just as you cannot think of long without short or short without long. Long is only long in comparison with short.

This warning against the mind's tendency to reify, to refer to processes as if they were things, parallels the Mahāyāna critique of a certain Hīnayāna interpretation of the Abhidharma. The Abhidharma took the idea of the *pudgala* or 'person' and broke it down into smaller elements known as *dharmas*. These *dharmas* were really a way of naming constituent processes within the overall 'being' of the person, but some of the Abhidharma scholastics tended to invest *dharmas* themselves with the same sort of reality that, in the case of the *pudgala*, they had used the *dharmas* to deny. There is little use in exorcising the idea of a person or a thing with the concept of process if that process is itself thought of as consisting of a succession of self-existent things. More than this, it is potentially harmful. To deny the existence of a 'self' while offering a world of self-existent entities is simply alienating, without that denial having any effect upon the deep-seated delusion of selfhood.

We have to use words
to release the world of our named experience
from the bonds that words themselves have forged.

Nāgārjuna's tactic throughout this section is to chip away at the idea of the self as something that really exists. He is giving the ego a hammering while at the same time denying that the object of his attack really exists. However, there is an inherent difficulty with this approach. The issue is one of the nature of concepts and how one employs them. In speaking of something whose existence one is endeavouring to disprove, one can end up strengthening, at a deeper, unconscious level, the sense of that thing as really existing.

Reification, or making things of processes, runs deep in the way we see ourselves and the world. We talk about someone having 'a problem with anger' or 'concentration difficulties' when in fact that person is just habitually angry or habitually inattentive. One who needs to change how they behave does not have something actually there to deal with called 'anger' or 'selfishness'. These are just words for ways in which energy is deployed. Anger occurs when energy is used in an unskilful way, whereas compassion or *mettā* occurs when energy is able to arise in skilful ways. Buddhism encourages us to think in terms of process or action, not in terms of things, objects, or entities. A person is not a living entity, a person is just living.

Any word used as a noun apparently refers to a thing. Words check the flow of experience, chopping it up into a series of material objects and mental states. This in turn places limits on what we are able to experience: language conditions experience. No doubt in its earliest, primitive phase, language subserved practical needs: 'Let's go and hunt,' 'Throw your spear,' 'Bring me that stone.' But when it comes to the communication of spiritual truths, the language of particular terms, attached to particular things, is simply unequal to the task. We have to learn to use language against the grain of its original purpose, which was to tie things down. We have to use words to release the world of our named experience from the bonds that words themselves have forged. As T.S. Eliot says, in 'East Coker',

Because one has only learnt to get the better of words
For the thing one no longer has to say,...

However, once we have realized that the terms we use refer to relative, conditioned processes, they can be put to effective use in helping us deal with the world, for useful they undoubtedly are, as Nāgārjuna goes on to point out. Notwithstanding the fact that 'cause' and 'effect' are provisional terms, and inadequate to describe what is really going on, we should nonetheless assert the conventional truth that they represent. Only if we take our stand upon this provisional truth and reject nihilism can we realize the absolute truth, asserting as true what 'does not arise from conventions'.

Nāgārjuna goes on to reinforce his central point with additional arguments, apparently deployed in order to meet various objections and referring, at least by implication, to various contemporary schools of thought, both Buddhist and non-Buddhist. The modern reader does not need to get bogged down in the details of these debates, as long as he or she bears in mind the central point: that the idea of a self is a fiction obscuring awareness of reality.

EMPTINESS AS TRANSCENDING
NIHILISM AND ETERNALISM

One who conceives of the mirage-like world
That it does or does not exist
Is consequently ignorant.
When there is ignorance, one is not liberated.

A follower of non-existence goes to bad transmigrations,
And a follower of existence goes to happy transmigrations.
Through correct and true knowledge
One does not rely on dualism and becomes liberated.[45]

For Nāgārjuna, a nihilist is one who believes that the mirage-like world does not really exist. He or she operates from a profoundly negative standpoint, refusing to accept that things are causally connected, arising in dependence upon definite conditions, and disappearing when those conditions are removed. Without this kind of connection the world has no sense or meaning, and spiritual practice becomes pointless. Nihilism is the philosophical expression of an attitude of aversion to the world. Aversion does, however, rely upon the existence of the thing that is disliked. If one hates the world so utterly as to deny its very existence, in the sense of regarding its operations as morally meaningless and life as ultimately futile, one is in fact asserting its existence quite strongly.

> It is better to be a relatively well-adjusted, forward-looking,
> ethical person, albeit with strong worldly attachments,
> than to be a critical, carping, sour, disillusioned,
> and world-rejecting cynical one.

It is this negative attitude that will lead to bad transmigrations, in other words to rebirth in unhappy realms. At root there is an unwillingness to engage with the world on its own terms. Denying its very existence leaves us free to do whatever we like. A nihilist does not believe that unskilful actions result in suffering, and it is this that makes nihilism so dangerous both to the individual and to society. The problem with nihilism is that, like other forms of negativity, it can present itself in pseudo-spiritual guise – like the view that 'all is one' and that, morally speaking, there is no difference between right and wrong. A person who is by temperament nihilistic may even be attracted to Buddhism by the idea of destroying the self or ego. But self-hatred or self-denial, far from helping one to overcome or see through the self, may actually reinforce one's deluded emotional investment in it.

The 'follower of existence', on the other hand, is an eternalist. Such a person believes that the world is no less real than it appears to be, that life has a meaning, and that other worlds, like heaven and hell, are also real. In consequence of this view, that person takes the way he or she lives in this world seriously, and tends to be ethically scrupulous. If the mental attitude of the nihilist is characterized by hatred, that of the eternalist is marked by attachment.

Attachment is by no means a positive mental state, but it is a step up from nihilism. You will not find liberation as an eternalist; you will continue to experience further rebirths, but the belief that the world really does exist, and that you can grasp things, and even keep hold of them, will tend to make those rebirths happy ones. It is better to be a relatively well-adjusted, forward-looking, ethical person, albeit with strong worldly attachments, than to be a critical, carping, sour, disillusioned, and world-rejecting cynical one. From the spiritual point of view, a healthy acceptance of the mundane is a more promising foundation for future spiritual development than is a complete rejection of life as it presents itself, even if that rejection comes armed with 'Buddhist' credentials.

Liberation, however, is something different from those two views. Enlightenment is an awakening from the view either that the mirage-like world is existent or that it is non-existent. One cannot say of a mirage that it exists in the sense of being absolutely real, nor can one say that it does not exist at all, since it is perceived. The same is true of the world. In this way, one goes beyond dualism.

SELF-MORTIFICATION AND ASCETIC TRAINING

Practice is not done by just
Mortifying the body,
For one has not forsaken injuring others
And is not helping others.

Those not esteeming the great path of excellent doctrine
Bright with giving, ethics, and patience,
Afflict their bodies, taking
An aberrant path like a cow path (deceiving oneself and those
* following).*

Their bodies embraced by the vicious snakes
Of the afflictive emotions, they enter for a long time
The dreadful jungle of cyclic existence
Among the trees of endless beings.[46]

Mortifying the body is an expression of the wrong view of nihilism. It arises from the association of the spiritual life with suffering, from the idea that pain does one good, and that suffering is the great purifier. The rationale underpinning this practice is that by mortifying the flesh one is able to bring bodily desires and instincts under control, and that by treating the body with aversion one distances oneself from it and ceases to identify with it. In reality, however, self-mortification succeeds only in placing the body as much at the centre of attention as does extreme sensual self-indulgence.

> We are happy to indulge ourselves, and we are happy to punish ourselves, but the middle way of self-discipline and spiritual training we find almost impossible to follow.

123

This mistaken rationale is understandable, given the central importance in Buddhism of the concept of *duḥkha*, suffering or unsatisfactoriness. But another way of looking at the Buddha's teaching about *duḥkha* is to reflect that he is simply reminding us that there is no point in imagining that discomfort and suffering can be avoided altogether. When they are unavoidable, one will best endure them if one does so with cheerful equanimity, rather than by trying to deny their existence, or seeking to distract oneself. The Buddha made it clear that the spiritual life is not necessarily a painful one. One type of disciple, he says, does indeed struggle all through their career: they never have an easy time. Another type has trouble to begin with but finds their practice more enjoyable as they go on. A third type begins practising with ease but runs into difficulties later. And there is a final type whose spiritual life starts off pleasantly and continues to be pleasant all the way through.

The issue is not quite so clear cut as it appears. For one thing, there is a disparity between the pleasant conditions that the ordinary person needs in order to enjoy a pleasant existence, and the often spartan conditions within which the spiritual practitioner is able to feel happy and joyful. One's experience of the spiritual life might be happy and inspired while appearing difficult and painful to people who have no wish to live that kind of life. Looking at those conditions from the outside, the ordinary person naturally imagines that the spiritual life must be tough and pretty joyless, and that any rewards were being paid for in advance with suffering. But the practitioner might well be experiencing inner contentment and joy, regardless of the external conditions.

The fact is that at certain key points in one's spiritual life there will probably be a degree of discomfort, not least because having to undo long-established habits of body, speech, and mind goes against the grain of human nature. But as one goes on, one's experience should become ever more joyful, whatever discomfort or difficult circumstances might be encountered. In any case, the experience of discomfort and suffering does not in itself signify that anything of a truly spiritual nature is happening. In my early days in England, after my return from India, I found this misapprehension rife among certain practitioners of Zen and 'vipassanā' meditation. Basically, they were punishing themselves and calling it Buddhism. The chief benchmark they used to determine their progress was the degree of mental and physical suffering they had experienced in connection with meditation. To judge by his oddly gloating manner, the monk who had instructed them in 'vipassanā' before my arrival seemed to relish their sufferings as much as they did themselves. When one of his disciples told me that I was not at all like him, I felt the remark was not really meant as a compliment. It was with a certain wistful admiration that she went on, 'He was a real sadist.'

It is understandable that people should go awry in this way, because many in the West tend to confuse an unhealthy desire for self-mortification, based on feelings of guilt, self-hatred, and self-contempt, with a healthy appreciation of the need for self-discipline. The word asceticism comes from the Greek word *askesis* which means simply 'training'. Just as the athlete trains the body, so the spiritual practitioner trains the mind. This is quite different from self-mortification, though it must be admitted that much of what passes for self-discipline is in fact neurotic self-mortification. It seems that we often find it easier to punish ourselves than to apply true self-discipline. We are happy to indulge ourselves, and we are happy to punish ourselves, but the middle way of self-discipline and spiritual training we find almost impossible to follow. This is partly because much of what is really simple self-discipline we tend to think of as a form of self-mortification. A person who eats meat, for example, is likely to regard giving it up as an act of self-denial rather than as a part of training.

125

The situation is further confused by the way occasional pleasures so easily turn into regular indulgences and even become indispensable in the end. Accustomed as we are to our comfortable beds, we would find making do with a mattress on the floor a real hardship. But for many people in the world who are used to sleeping on a mat on the ground, a mattress would be the height of luxury. The truth is that almost everyone in the West today enjoys a level of luxury and comfort that would not have been within the reach of even the wealthiest a few hundred years ago.

Training is therefore a question of loosening the ties that bind us to whatever comforts we have got used to, doing without them from time to time, and, most important of all, doing so cheerfully. A footballer is happy to train for six hours a day, a concert pianist to practise for eight hours a day. They are not punishing themselves. They are doing the training in order to achieve their particular objective. That is all. For the spiritual ascetic it is no different. If you want to help your team score goals – in the spiritual life as much as on the football pitch – you have to put in the training.

Nāgārjuna puts his finger on the nub of the matter when he points out that self-mortification is useless as regards the broad aims of the spiritual life. In putting energy into afflicting the body we are signalling our lack of interest in any real spiritual endeavour, and Nāgārjuna goes on to specify what it is that, at the most basic level of Mahāyāna endeavour, we are choosing not to practise: the first three perfections – giving, ethics, and patience. It is our failure to appreciate the positive nature of the spiritual path that allows us to adopt this harmful and useless approach. Far from leading to liberation, self-mortification only binds more tightly to conditioned existence. By punishing yourself for your indulgences, you become more deeply attached to them. I should add that tormenting oneself mentally is a modern variation of this. If in your attempts to live a spiritual life you become anxious, make yourself wretched, and insist on working yourself into a state of exhaustion, something has clearly gone wrong. It is unfortunately not uncommon for people to use their idea of the spiritual life, unconsciously and compulsively, as a means of giving themselves or others a hard time. You don't really know you're doing it, or why you're doing it, but you can't help looking for suffering of some kind, even from the Dharma, which is the means of putting an end to anguish. If you do this, if you deliberately invite suffering in the context of your spiritual life in one way or another, then your spiritual life isn't really functioning as a means of liberation.

Self-hatred can be difficult to dislodge if it stems from childhood experiences. Those from whom we learn about ourselves and the world in our early years pass on to us, knowingly or unknowingly, attitudes that we imbibe with our mother's milk, so to speak. At that early stage in our development, we do not question those attitudes, and consequently we take them in deeply, so deeply that they sometimes stay with us for the rest of our lives. If we were given the message that we were inadequate or bad, in any situation later in life where things do not turn out as we would have liked, we naturally assume that this is owing to our inadequacy or our wickedness, because that was how we were taught to interpret any unpleasant experience.

If you are a person with this kind of mentality, you might imagine that you were leading a balanced spiritual life even though, at the same time, you were rejecting such practices as the *mettā bhāvanā* as being 'too positive'. Presented with the sort of practice that would do you the most good, you will object that you just can't get on with it, it doesn't suit your particular needs. This is where you need spiritual friends, because it is inevitable that your deepest compulsions are going to resist the change which, consciously, you are trying to make. That resistance will cunningly co-opt your spiritual efforts for its own purposes and use them to establish itself even more firmly if friends are not on hand to support a more helpful pattern of practice.

MINDFULNESS AND INTOXICATION

Not drinking intoxicants …[47]

There is of course a much more down-to-earth aspect of ethical practice in relation to the mind. In the *Precious Garland*, having listed the ten precepts, Nāgārjuna raises an issue that has become a major social problem these days, at least in some countries: drink. To which we can add the closely related issue of drugs. There is a clear analogy here with sex, in that sex, like drink and drugs, can be addictive, though one form of intoxication is purely psychological whereas the other is both psychological and chemical.

> A rather deliberate, cool, and formal manner
> is sometimes taken as a sign of mindfulness,
> whereas in fact true mindfulness is relaxed
> and emotionally warm, even expansive.

The Buddhist tradition rules out indulgence in intoxicating substances altogether. The last of the five ethical precepts taken by Buddhists refers to this. However, the fact that in the list of the ten precepts this fifth precept is replaced by extra speech and mind-training precepts suggests that the latter is meant more as a safeguard against any loss of mindfulness and awareness. It may be that we can take a slightly more liberal attitude towards intoxicants, so long as we can see some real benefit in doing so. The question is basically one of mindfulness, and mindfulness involves above all being aware of one's thoughts and emotions.

A rather deliberate, cool, and formal manner is sometimes taken as a sign of mindfulness, whereas in fact true mindfulness is relaxed and emotionally warm, even expansive. As it is difficult to be truly mindful when one is tense or self-conscious, there may be situations in which a glass of wine will promote relaxation. I found this to be the case in the early days of the Friends of the Western Buddhist Order, when from time to time I invited a few people round for a meal. A bottle of wine would loosen up the painfully stiff, inhibited atmosphere that sometimes prevailed on these occasions. Clearly such tactics are only a means to an end, and they should not be allowed to become a habit, and although a glass of wine may help, it does not follow that three or four glasses will help even more.

> People who drink regularly desire such confusion.
> They fear clarity and some even long for oblivion.

Drinking alcohol eventually leads to mental confusion, so one can only conclude that people who drink regularly *desire* such confusion. They fear clarity and some even long for oblivion. They drink to forget, at least to forget themselves, to take the sharp edge off painful feelings, to relieve pressure. And it works up to a point, at least temporarily. Thus begins the downward spiral of addiction. We therefore have to address our emotional needs somewhere other than at the bottom of a glass, because once drink takes hold, clarity – including moral clarity – slips away. Once you are addicted you will do pretty well anything to satisfy your craving.

Intoxicants lead to worldly scorn,
Your affairs are ruined, wealth is wasted,
The unsuitable is done from delusion,
Therefore always avoid intoxicants.

Gambling causes avarice,
Unpleasantness, hatred, deception, cheating,
Wildness, lying, senseless talk, and harsh speech,
Therefore always avoid gambling.[48]

129

More worldly advice: no one respects a drunkard or a drug addict. Such a person neglects their worldly affairs, since their time is spent either indulging their habit or recovering from the effects of the indulgence. Even in Nāgārjuna's day, getting drunk seems to have been an expensive business. Moreover, a drunkard does stupid things; he loses his inhibitions, and all sense of what is appropriate and seemly. The 'unsuitable' is indeed done. In these and many other ways intoxicants lay waste one's life.

There is quite a lot of advice of this sort in ancient Buddhist texts, suggesting that the people of India used to be rather more given to drink than they are today. These days, at least among unwesternized Indians, drinking alcohol is regarded as being utterly disreputable, especially in the case of religious practitioners.

As for gambling, a host of evils is said to follow in its wake. You become obsessed with money (or its equivalent), regardless of whether you are winning or losing. Money is, after all, the centre of interest in gambling. You also crave the feeling of elation that comes from winning, elation being a kind of drug, but more often than not there is the deflation that comes when you lose your money, together with the resentment you feel towards those to whom you have lost it. You will do anything in order to win: you will cheat and deceive. You lose control of yourself in your rage to win and your fury at losing. And you lie to your family about where the money has gone.

There is also an element of self-deception in the way we justify our addictions, whether it is to drink or drugs or gambling. We believe that we are in control. Similarly, we try to justify the addictions of others. For example, some defend bingo halls, bars, and pubs on the grounds that they are places of harmless enjoyment that promote social interaction, and no one, they say, has the right to object to the perfectly legal pleasures and amusements of other people. However, the fact is that bingo is gambling, while pubs and bars tend to encourage alcoholism. Drinking and gambling do indeed have the kind of effects that Nāgārjuna itemizes. If they are the only 'social' activities in which many people engage, that is sad, but why this should be so is another matter entirely.

CRAVING, HATRED, AND DELUSION

Covetousness destroys one's wishes,
Harmful intent yields fright,
Wrong views lead to bad views,
And drink to confusion of the mind.[49]

As ever, Nāgārjuna doesn't beat about the bush. He spells out for the king the consequences of not observing the three mind precepts. The result of covetousness, he says, is not that you get what you want, but rather that you get what you don't want, the nature of craving being such that once the desired object is obtained, it often ceases to be desired. As Oscar Wilde famously put it, 'In this world there are only two tragedies. One is not getting what one wants, and the other is getting it.'[50] Especially when we have set our heart on some very special object, we may well find, on finally getting possession of it, that we have invested it with qualities it does not really have. Whether it is an experience, an article, or a person – success, a car, a lover – we find, when we've got it, that it is not after all what we wanted. By that time, though, it is probably too late to change our mind; we've got it – or we've married it – and have to deal with the responsibilities and demands that such possession brings. And we are no more contented than we were before.

We have been warned that killing brings a short life, and that harming brings suffering. Now we are told that the intent to harm brings fear. These are all variations on the same theme, one that is of particular relevance to a ruler or, in fact, to any-one with power over others. For such people, 'harmful intent' is often associated with consolidating their position and neutralizing those who might threaten them. Nāgārjuna reminds his royal disciple that the fruit of such an intent is not security but its opposite: fear. If your days and nights are spent scheming to harm others, you will be living in a fearful, dangerous world. Putting it more psychologically, we may say that hatred produces paranoia, which is our own projected hatred reflected back to us. With paranoia, the fear is largely unfounded, and the hatred largely unconscious. The experience of paranoia tells us less about the real attitude of other people towards us than it does about our own unacknowledged emotions. Similarly, the feeling of victimization, the sense that others are out to get one, often comes from our unacknowledged ill will towards those who, we imagine, dislike us and wish to harm us.

This is paranoia as projection. In a way, it arises naturally out of the fact that people tend to hate those who hate them. Thus if you hate someone, you are likely to think that they hate you. You interpret everything they do or say as a sign that they are plotting against you. Absolute rulers can easily slip into this way of perceiving the world around them. Victims of paranoia weave complex webs of 'evidence' to support their fantasies, while those of whom they are so crazily suspicious are guilty only of wondering why someone is looking at them in such a strange manner.

To say that wrong views lead to wrong views (presumably what is meant by 'bad views') is tantamount to saying that there is nothing worse than wrong views. No other affliction can match the bane of wrong views. Hell itself is not so much the deserved consequence of wrong views as is falling into further wrong views. Wrong views lead inexorably to more wrong views. Their nature is to breed. Once you embrace a wrong view, you sink more and more deeply into the morass of mere opinions and speculations.

Nor should we hold too tightly even to right views. The Buddha regarded all views, even those that were practically helpful and therefore 'right', as having only a limited value as compared with the experience of Enlightenment. Once you regard a particular view not just as a provisionally held position, or as something to reflect on, but as being unconditionally true, it ceases to function as right view. A right view to which you cling, a right view you turn into a totem, becomes to that extent a wrong view.

Afraid of the fearless abode,
Ruined, they ruin others.
O King, act in such a way
That the ruined do not ruin you.[51]

'Ruined' might seem a strong word to use in this connection, but it reminds us of just what is at stake when we embark on the spiritual life. We face ruin if we 'back' the wrong view and views, moreover, can be contagious. Our own particular view of the world has been 'caught' from our experience of the world, especially the society in which we live. Those with whom we associate will constantly give off, with everything they say and do, a view of themselves and of others and of the world around them. We should therefore be careful about our choice of associates, as well as careful about how we ourselves affect others. In view of the fact that we are very rarely aware of being 'ruined' ourselves when such is the case, what Nāgārjuna is saying suggests that a certain watchfulness, a certain modesty and reticence, is always appropriate in our dealings with others lest they be 'ruined' through their association with us.

CULTIVATING THE MIND

Through not wavering you will attain mindfulness,
Through thinking you will attain intelligence.
Through respect you will be endowed with realization of meaning,
Through guarding the doctrine you will become wise.[52]

Through overcoming mental distraction, you clearly will become more aware. When you are distracted, different parts of you are pulling in different directions, so to speak, and the communication between them breaks down, so that at that time you have very little overall awareness. If you can stabilize your thoughts, more of you will be present in what you say and do.

Next we come to how we apply this awareness, once it has been established. By thinking is meant creative thinking – specifically, the investigation of mental states. For most of us, thinking often involves anxiety, as when we worry about what is going to happen to us when we are old. For Nāgārjuna, intelligence consists in developing a clearer understanding of the true nature of our situation. It means bringing awareness into our thinking. It is directed thought, mindful thought, especially the mindful observation of our own mental processes.

> Questioning the wise should be
> an extension of questioning ourselves.

If the mind is not used, the faculty of intelligence tends to atrophy. And we often use our minds more creatively when we ask questions, rather than when we assume we know the answers. Asking questions can take many forms: intelligent reading, for example, can be a matter of asking questions. When you open a book, perhaps out of curiosity, as when you are intrigued by the title, this too can be indicative of a questioning attitude. You are approaching the book with a mind of your own rather than just absorbing its contents like a piece of blotting paper.

The kind of questions you ask makes a difference. If you use your intelligence to ask only about mundane things, you are, in effect, excluding the possibility of any spiritual understanding. However cleverly your questions may be put, they will lead you gradually into a state of delusion in which there is no awareness of anything beyond what the senses convey. It is a matter of where your real interests lie. The spiritual life itself is a kind of interrogation of reality. This does not mean cross-examining the wise, or calling into question or impuging the wise. Nor is it a matter of asking questions without first thinking for oneself. Questioning the wise should be an extension of questioning ourselves. I would also say that we should not question the wise just in order to sound off, or to gain confirmation of our own opinions. That said, there are people who are not very assertive and who do not have many opportunities to say what they think and feel. When they find themselves with someone who is prepared to listen, they might feel they have at last been given permission to express themselves, and that is no bad thing, even if what they have to say is not very relevant. Questioning the wise does indeed mean being open to the wise, but there are people who need to experience someone who is prepared to be open to them before they can be open in their turn.

Even a sharp intelligence is not enough, however. By 'respect' is meant something more like 'reverence', and this positive quality, too, is needed. One needs, that is, a certain receptivity to higher things as well as the kind of attitude that comes with reverence. I would go so far as to say that without a measure of receptivity, and even of sympathy, you will not really understand anything, even intellectually, over and above mere facts. Such forms of emotional resistance as prejudice and defensiveness prevent us from being open to even ordinary knowledge, let alone open to higher spiritual truths. Respect or reverence involves an attitude of interest and openness and a warm, engaged curiosity. It is a readiness to learn. Without it we will distort or misrepresent whatever we engage with intellectually, whether the Dharma or anything else.

This attitude is to be cultivated not just towards the Dharma, but also towards members of the Sangha or spiritual community. We should always approach another individual with

135

respect, whatever their level of spiritual development. There should always be sympathy between members of the spiritual community – that is, a real desire to understand what another person is saying or is endeavouring to express. One does not have to agree, but we should try to see other people objectively, and do our best to imagine what it might be like to be in their shoes. Without receptivity we cannot understand another person, however shrewd and sharp we may be. Respect for others involves an appreciation of the fact that our understanding of them is a limited one.

Having taken in the meaning of the Dharma, we have to retain it if we are to 'become wise'. In other words, we do not become wise simply by understanding the Dharma; we become wise by bearing it in mind, pondering it, not allowing ourselves to forget it. When we understand something or even get a flash of insight, it might seem at the time that we've got it for good. Yet we lose it. We lose it because we do or think or talk about other things, and fail to allow the time necessary for assimilation. The deeper the insight, the more time we may need to devote to its contemplation.

For anyone who leads a busy life, making notes is an essential element in this process. When you come back to them months or years later, you will often realize how little you have remembered. You find that points which made a deep impression on you at the time have left no trace in your mind. You might find it useful to make notes on your meditation, your reading, group study, or even on a serious talk with a friend. Sometimes just a few words will be enough to allow you to go back to an earlier insight and turn it over in your mind at your leisure. Coming back to your notes, you might also notice that you now understand them better. If you do not write things down, you will certainly lose the insight, especially in the earliest stages of its development. The phone rings, and when the call is over you might not even remember that you had

136

been thinking at all. Personally, I wish that in my earlier days I had written down much more than I did.

A meditation notebook is useful in that it enables you to follow the ups and downs of your practice from week to week and month to month. You will notice perhaps that you have not done the *mettā bhāvanā* for a month, or that you have your best meditations around the time of the full moon. And when you hit a difficult patch, and start thinking you were not cut out for meditation, you can go through your notebook and find evidence to the contrary. Your mood, or even a passing negative attitude, might have deleted your more positive experiences from your memory. A notebook acts like an observant intimate friend who remembers everything you tell them.

Through the concentrations, immeasurables, and formlessnesses
One experiences the bliss of Brahmā and so forth.
Thus in brief are the practices
For high status and their fruits.[53]

The immeasurables are four meditation practices which involve the cultivation of positive emotion. They are also known, more poetically, as the four *brahma vihāras*, the 'divine abidings'. These are loving-kindness or *maitrī* (*mettā*), compassion or *karuṇā*, sympathetic joy or *muditā*, and equanimity or *upekṣā* (*upekkhā*). The rather cumbersome 'formlessnesses' refers to the four formless absorptions, the *arūpa dhyānas*: the experience or knowledge of the spheres of infinite space, infinite consciousness, no-thing-ness, and neither perception nor non-perception. Nāgārjuna is speaking of the successively higher superconscious states brought about by the practice of meditation, states which take one to the corresponding heavenly or *deva* realms of traditional Buddhist cosmology. These higher states can be experienced not only during this life, when one practises meditation; they can also be experienced after death when one is reborn in the heavenly realm corresponding to one's meditative attainment during one's lifetime. The heavenly realms into which one might be reborn are not eternal; even there one is still on the wheel of becoming. This is also true when one enters these realms in meditation. One may enter a heavenly realm, in the sense of having an experience of peace and bliss and spiritual renewal, but one will still be within conditioned existence unless one has the determination to pass beyond it into the still higher, transcendental realm of Enlightenment.

This fleeting reference to meditation
in the context of skilful actions and their consequences
reminds us that meditation is a form of action.

Of course, there is a clear difference between the idea that meditation leads to states of bliss and the idea that skilful actions lead to worldly prosperity, the former being verifiable in experience whereas with the latter this is not the case. Meditative absorption, once achieved, offers a direct experience of relaxation and tranquillity, whereas the karmic fruits of a virtuous life have to be taken on trust as something we can look forward to in the future, whether in this life or in a future existence. After all, honesty does not always pay. As the Bible says, the wicked man does sometimes 'flourish like the bay tree'.[54] His victims seem only too often to experience the sufferings which under the law of karma are rightly his. It might be comforting to think that the rich are miserable and unable to enjoy their ill-gotten gains. But is this true? Does the swindler really lie awake at night worrying about losing the money that he has obtained fraudulently, or is this just a consoling fantasy on the part of those of us who tread a more honest path? Whatever the truth of this – and we cannot really know – connecting the spiritual life with worldly gains, whether those gains are real or imagined, whether they constitute psychological well-being or a better life in the future, inevitably distracts us from the real purpose of spiritual practice.

This fleeting reference to meditation in the context of skilful actions and their consequences reminds us that meditation is a form of action. All thoughts are actions. Positive thought *is* skilful action. It is easy to imagine that in practising meditation you are not really doing anything, but the truth is that meditation is a powerful thing, in that it is productive of important consequences for the meditator. An action will always produce some kind of result. (If no result is produced, it means that nothing has been done.) A thought, inasmuch as it constitutes an intention, produces a karmic result even if it is not acted upon immediately. It changes us to some degree, or at least begins to take us in a certain direction. The result, in the case of meditation, is more than simply a shift of emphasis among existing mental and emotional elements. When one meditates with conviction something quite new is generated and this contributes to one's spiritual development.

6

MENTAL STATES

Having analysed well
All deeds of body, speech, and mind,
Those who realize what benefit self and others
And always perform these are wise.[55]

This verse makes it clear that the full realization of what benefits oneself and others comes from cultivating mindfulness, from 'having analysed well all deeds of body, speech, and mind' – that is, from being keenly aware at any given moment of whether what you are doing is beneficial or harmful. This aspect of mindfulness is sometimes called *dharma-vicaya*, the investigation of mental states (*dharma* here meaning a mental state), and it is an important part of Buddhist practice. In it, one constantly examines oneself, scrutinizing one's deeds of body, speech, and mind, and judging as far as one can whether they are skilful or unskilful, whether they have been prompted by kindness and wisdom or by craving, hatred, and delusion. In more general terms, the skilful is whatever pertains to the path and to the goal, whether directly or indirectly;

while the unskilful is that which takes one off the path and out of sight of the goal.

Mindfulness is not a question
of somehow standing outside one's experience
and observing it.

Here we are presented with another way of viewing ethical practice. But will such constant evaluation of our mental states not detract from our spontaneity? If you are forever stopping and analysing what you are thinking, doing, and saying, are you not adopting a rather mechanical and even alienating attitude to your experience? Will it not make you too self-conscious to be able to live authentically? There is another question, which needs to be dealt with first: is it, in fact, true spontaneity that we value, or do we simply want to indulge instinctive and reactive behaviour? After all, our negative instincts and destructive habits are no less spontaneous than our creative impulses. If we just want to give free rein to all our different energies, we might as well forget about practising mindfulness.

This granted, it is nonetheless essential to stay in contact with the springs of one's creativity. Somehow you have to strike a balance between giving so much free rein to your instincts and energies that you lose all hope of being able to bring mindfulness to bear on them and being so self-analytical that you simply inhibit and stultify yourself. Here, the challenge is to be active and spontaneous and, at the same time, aware and mindful, so that there is a single mental and spiritual process in which awareness and spontaneity are indistinguishable. This is what happens when you are absorbed in work, for example: all your energy is going into the work, yet at the same time you are very aware of what you are doing. With artistic or creative work, especially, is this the case. A unification of spontaneity and awareness can also take place in the course of human communication, when a real exchange of thoughts and feelings starts to flow between two people. It can happen in a crisis, or in a moment of danger, when all your energies are mobilized to meet an overwhelming challenge.

Mindfulness demands the ability to immerse oneself in one's experience whilst at the same time being conscious of the nature of that experience. It is not a cold, objective, intellectual process, not a question of somehow standing outside one's experience and observing it. The awareness should infuse and inform the action, or the speech, or even the thought. It should do so, moreover, with a strong element of positive feeling, even joy.

> You do not need to tear yourself up by the roots
> every few minutes to see if you have grown a little.

Mindfulness means that one is better able to decide whether or not to do something. If you are naturally a cautious, inhibited, self-controlled kind of person, you might try seeing what would happen if you were just to let rip. For some people mindfulness might mean unbuttoning a little, taking a risk and following a spontaneous impulse as a way of weakening their inhibitions. If, on the other hand, you are rather wild by nature, and tend to be spontaneous in a purely instinctual and reactive way, mindfulness would involve restraining yourself and learning to curb your reactivity.

Dharma-vicaya does not mean breaking the flow of life by stopping at every turn in order to assess yourself according to some abstract notion of spiritual progress. It is simply a general awareness of how *relatively* skilful or unskilful any given action, thought, or utterance is, a sense of the extent to which you are moving towards a positive goal. You do not need to tear yourself up by the roots every few minutes to see if you have grown a little. Rather you can make a start with *dharma-vicaya* by taking stock of yourself from time to time, in order to ascertain the general direction of your actions of body, speech, and mind. Are they expressive of greed, hatred, and mental confusion, or expressive of generosity, kindness, and understanding? Then at some point you need to embark upon the systematic development of moment-by-moment mindfulness, and become more aware of your mental states as they arise, as well as aware of the direction in which any given mental state is heading. In this way you will ensure that your confidence in what you are doing is sustained and that all the things you think and do and say contribute to the attainment of your goal.

With practice, the analysis can become more searching. It is *dharma-vicaya* that leads to wisdom, not theoretical knowledge. Generally speaking we understand intellectually far more than we are capable of putting into practice. After all, it is not so very difficult to take stock of one's actions of body, speech, and mind and judge whether or not they benefit oneself and others. But this is not enough. One has to live by the light of that knowledge. When it comes to putting what we know into practice, all sorts of conditions other than intellectual understanding, particularly habits, come into play. It is only by studying our actions and thoughts in detail, moment by moment, and seeing their effect upon us directly, that we will start to break down our habitual ways of responding to the world.

FIRST, FORSAKE ANGER

Then having become a monastic
You should first be intent on the training (in ethics).
You should endeavour at the discipline of individual liberation,
At hearing frequently, and delineating their meaning.

Then, you should forsake
These which are called assorted faults.
With vigour you should definitely realize
Those renowned as the fifty-seven.

Belligerence is a disturbance of mind.
Enmity is a (tight) hanging onto that.
Concealment is a hiding of ill-deeds (when confronted).
Malevolence is to cling to ill-deeds.[56]

Here Nāgārjuna recommends that the new monk should follow what I call the Path of Regular Steps.[57] However lofty and altruistic your goal, at the beginning of your spiritual career you have to start by working on yourself, devoting yourself to your own 'individual liberation'. No doubt by getting on with your personal practice you will have a positive effect upon others, but unless you gain a degree of insight, you will not be able to help them more radically. It might seem selfish just to persist with your own practice of meditation rather than teaching others, but in the long run it is the depth of your meditative experience that is going to help you communicate the Dharma most effectively. Note that Nāgārjuna is recommending taking up not the *ideal* of individual liberation (i.e. the Arhant ideal), but simply the *discipline* of individual liberation (i.e. the *prātimokṣa*). The ideal remains that of the Mahāyāna, not of the Hīnayāna, but for the time at least being your discipline is that of individual liberation. In the same way, while true spontaneity may be your ideal, your present discipline might have to be quite strict, even narrow, if you are to achieve that ideal in the long run.

> Mundane freedom may in the end feel like bondage,
> just as material wealth may feel like poverty.

There follows a touch of the Abhidharma, with a list of fifty-seven unskilful mental states.[58] It is not enough just to recognize the existence of these states in us; we have to bring mindfulness to bear on them. The purpose of our taking this long hard look at the unskilful tendencies of our own mind is so that we may take steps to eradicate them and thus become, eventually, free from them.

Anger comes first, because it is from anger that resentment, hatred, and enmity all arise. Being the direct opposite of the Bodhisattva's compassionate vow, these states are the most unskilful that we can experience. Anger is of a momentary and explosive nature, often being the result of a build-up of frustrated energy. You want something but you cannot get it, or you want to say something but you cannot say it. Eventually you explode. Resentment or hatred is a more settled anger, the result of brooding over one's wrongs, real or imagined, so that one's mind is slowly poisoned. Enmity goes even further, being the persistent desire to harm another person. While hatred is a mental attitude, enmity consists in attempting actually to harm the object of your aversion, even over a period of years.

It has been said that hatred is the experience of pain, accompanied by the idea of an external cause. Hatred arises from the natural impulse to remove or counteract the person you have identified as the cause of your suffering, though they might not be responsible for it, or even aware of the fact that you think them responsible. But some hatred is gratuitous. Such hatred is termed malice, the delight in inflicting suffering on others for its own sake, regardless of whether they have done you any harm. Thus there is a hierarchy of negative emotions consisting of anger, hatred, enmity, and malice.

Surprisingly enough, the greatest hatred often occurs between people who are supposedly very close to one another, between children and parents, between husband and wife, between people of the same religious tradition, and even between members of the same spiritual community. But these are the very people from whom we normally receive the most, emotionally speaking, and from whom we therefore expect the most. Bitter disappointment is thus more than likely. Another example is that of the welfare state, which was set up in Britain after the Second World War, and which has given rise to a great deal of resentment. People have been gradually conditioned into thinking that everything should be provided for them. When it is not, or when what is provided is not to their liking, they feel they have been cheated of what was due to them and become correspondingly angry.

A lot of resentment and unfocused anger comes from having everything you really need and yet still feeling deprived. This frustration and disappointment with a quite comfortable life is perhaps largely to do with spiritual deprivation. With no pressing material or physical needs, people are very quickly brought up against the basic question of what life itself is for, but without their having any real guidance on the subject. Our society has given us everything, without telling us how to make the best use of it. The innumerable petty regulations imposed by the government irritate people and breed resentment. Mundane freedom may in the end feel like bondage, just as material wealth may feel like poverty. No wonder people feel angry and hard done by. The trouble is that Utopia, which used to be in the future, has arrived now. If before the Second World War you had told the average working-class man or woman – especially the men in the long dole queues I saw in the 1930s – that in the future they would have a house of their own, a car, a television, new clothes every six months, a refrigerator and a washing machine, exotic ready-made meals and foreign holidays, and all for only five days' work each week, they would have said, 'That will be heaven. What more could you want?' But it has not worked out like that. People feel cheated of the happiness that should have been theirs. They feel cheated because they have got what they were promised without the happiness they assumed would accompany it.

The opposite of anger is patience, the capacity to endure difficulties or unpleasant situations without falling into, or expressing, negative emotions. Expressions like 'My patience snapped,' which ought to be a confession of weakness, are more often meant to be self-exculpatory, as if no one could be expected to be patient beyond a certain point. Initially, one who takes the practice of ethics seriously will feel disappointed, even frustrated, when hatred, or craving, or jealousy arises. You now know the harm these emotions can do, and yet they keep on arising. Rather than allowing yourself to be discouraged by this, you should remind yourself that the fact that you can recognize them for what they are means that you are on the way to overcoming them. If you indulge them, living with them easily, and if you ignore their malign influence, you are inviting them to arise again in the future. But if you can see them for what they are, you should also be able to see that simply berating yourself on their account only makes things worse. Gradually, you will learn how to deal with these negative emotions as soon as they arise.

For example, an angry thought, or even a spontaneous outburst of anger, is not necessarily a breach of your promise to generate compassion in place of ill will. In all likelihood you did not deliberately make yourself angry; the anger simply erupted owing to a long-standing lack of attention to your mental condition, possibly allied to a fiery temper. The promise is broken when you indulge anger and make no effort to eradicate it. If you take no positive steps to overcome it when it arises, you are in effect encouraging it to do so again. At bottom, anger is the product of frustrated desire, so a simpler lifestyle, if it is embraced happily, should have the effect of making anger and hatred less likely to arise.

Because hatred is intimately linked with craving or covetousness, it is always worth looking for its roots in frustrated desire. To take an obvious example, the nagging, restless itch of sexual craving can disturb our emotional balance, rob us of our peace of mind, and leave us discontented at best, and at worst full of jealous fury. Unfortunately, contemporary popular culture offers a constant invitation to indulge our many cravings, including sexual craving, and a spiritual practitioner has therefore all the more need to observe the ethical precepts. But if we are genuinely to observe them, we have to be able to find interest and pleasure and beauty elsewhere than in the objects of craving.

Bringing an element of friendliness and concern into our personal relationships can provide a degree of genuine emotional sustenance, the lack of which often lies at the root of our frustration and bitterness. Much of the time, what we are really looking for is this kind of sustenance. Another approach is the aesthetic one: the more our emotions are engaged with, and refined by poetry and the fine arts or by devotional practices, the less likely it is that we will be troubled by the grosser forms of craving and hatred. The key is to broaden and deepen our interests, to cultivate contentment, and to adopt a more aesthetic attitude to life. Admire the 'flower in the crannied wall' by all means, but be aware of your desire to pluck it out of the crannies, and without ceasing to appreciate its beauty, relax and relinquish your desire to possess it.

THE MANY FACES OF PRIDE

Arrogance is haughtiness (due to wealth, and so forth).
Non-conscientiousness is non-application at virtues.
Pride has seven forms
Each of which I will explain.

Fancying that one is lower than the lowly,
Or equal with the equal,
Or greater than or equal to the lowly –
All are called the pride of selfhood.

Boasting that one is equal to those
Who by some good quality are superior to oneself
Is called exceeding pride. Fancying that one is superior to the
superior,

Thinking that one is higher than the very high,
Is pride beyond pride;
Like sores on an abscess
It is very vicious.

Conceiving an I through obscuration
In the five empty (aggregates)
Which are called the appropriation
Is said to be the pride of thinking I.

Thinking one has won fruits (of the spiritual path)
Not yet attained is pride of conceit.
Praising oneself for faulty deeds
Is known by the wise as erroneous pride.

Deriding oneself, thinking
'I am useless,' is called
The pride of inferiority.
Such is a brief description of the seven prides.[59]

Success is always dangerous. From a spiritual point of view, failure has its rewards, but worldly success tends to produce what the ancient Greeks called hubris, the pride that comes before a fall. Thoughtless or unmindful pride brings inflation, the sense that you can do nothing wrong. You become careless; you think nothing can stand in your way. When this happens you will either have your inflated ego abruptly punctured, or it will suffer a slow, gradual deflation. Either way, you will be brought down to earth, and this will make you angry. You will think you were brought down by people who were jealous of you and your success, who could not bear their own comparative mediocrity. In this way you become more and more blind to what is really going on, and even when you have achieved something worthwhile, this blindness can detract from the positive nature of the achievement.

> People will take pride in almost anything
> that might bring them a little attention,
> even if that attention is far from flattering.

Haughtiness is thinking a lot of oneself and adopting a posture of superiority towards others, whereas arrogance goes further, and involves trying to force people to recognize that superiority. In some societies, for example in the old Tibet, arrogance and haughtiness seem to have been considered positive qualities. When some of my Tibetan friends in Kalimpong wanted to speak well of an aristocratic lady, for example, they would say in tones of admiration, 'She's really haughty!' as if haughtiness were the crowning virtue.

When pride includes self-denigration we have to broaden the meaning of the term. Insisting on being equal to others is pride. Even humility, if it is at all self-conscious, is pride. According to Nāgārjuna, belief in a separate unchanging self is pride. Any way in which we fix or inflate our sense of self, or separate ourselves from others by thinking that we are someone special, is pride.

You can be proud of a quality you have, you can be proud of a quality you do not have but think you have, and you can be proud of a quality you pretend you have. You might be genuinely learned, or enjoy an effective meditation practice, or even experience a degree of insight – all these can be accompanied by arrogance or inflation. You might, on the other hand, genuinely believe yourself to be Enlightened, say, or that you were a great painter, when in fact you were nothing of the kind. You might even allow people to believe you possessed certain spiritual attainments when you knew you did not really have them. All this is pride.

People will take pride in almost anything that might bring them a little attention, even if that attention is far from flattering. Some are proud of being good liars or successful cheats, or of how drunk they can get. Others are proud of being useless, at least in certain respects. The latter may be dressed up as self-deprecation. Such people will say, 'I'm afraid I'm absolutely hopeless at anything technical,' with a rather boastful air, as if to say, 'My mind is on higher things.'

Pride is about measuring ourselves against others, and it might seem that, ideally, we should not compare ourselves with others at all. However, we can hardly avoid doing so; we need to compare our abilities with those of other people from time to time, for various purposes. But comparisons can be made skilfully or unskilfully. An unskilful comparison consists in being neurotically concerned to find a place for oneself in relation to others in order to feel secure. You are anxious to know where you stand, whether you are equal, inferior, or superior to others. You might insist on being equal because really you feel insecure and in fact are constantly comparing yourself with others to your own detriment. A more positive form of comparison would be to ascertain where you stood in relation to others for the purpose of mutual growth and communication and to achieve common objectives. Regarding someone as inferior to you does not necessarily mean that you look down on them. It could mean that you recognize that you can do more for them than they can do for you. Conversely, looking up to someone need not mean that you grovel.

Boasting consists in overemphasizing one's own abilities in relation to those of others. Usually it is simply a case of saying, 'He may a better carpenter than I am, but *I'm* better at public speaking,' and a little awareness should prevent us from making too much of such relative advantages. Sometimes one person might be obviously superior to another in a general way, but given a change in circumstances the situation can be swiftly reversed. In J.M. Barrie's play *The Admirable Crichton*, a group of aristocrats are shipwrecked on a desert island, and the eponymous manservant shows himself to be vastly superior to everyone else in the party.

It is obvious that the Buddha was superior to the notorious bandit Aṅgulimāla, for example.[60] Even so, it needs to be made clear that banditry is not the point of comparison between them, for this would make Aṅgulimāla better than the

151

Buddha! That aside, we can say with confidence that the Buddha was a better man than Aṅgulimāla. However, as soon as Aṅgulimāla becomes Enlightened the difference between them immediately becomes much less. Comparisons of this kind are thus, if not odious, at least otiose. At one time you might be in a position to help a particular person; at another time, it might be you who needs the help and they who give it. There are always inequalities between people, and these need to be acknowledged if there is to be mutual helpfulness, but in the end they are not what matters most.

Nowadays the general attitude towards the comparison of one person with another is rather strange. On the one hand, a professional has his or her performance judged and measured against that of other professionals; on the other, there is widespread resistance to the idea that one person might be better than another in a more general way. The truth is that we should go down on our knees in gratitude to the Buddhas and Bodhisattvas for the fact that we are *not* superior to all others, and that there are some people who are far better than we are at the vital business of being human. If there are those to whom we can look up, there is hope for us in our own future development, as well as help. Pride can also be collective. It can take the form of nationalism, for example, which is an extension of the pride of the individual, the pride that says 'I'. Pride is a versatile, many-sided 'fault', and it is hardly to be expected that one will altogether escape it this side of Enlightenment.

Pride is not always negative. As a positive quality it comes under the heading of *apatrāpya* (*ottappa* in Pāli): conscience or self-respect. This kind of pride, radically transformed, is an important element in the Vajrayāna. There the practitioner is recommended to think, 'How can I, being in my essential nature a Buddha, behave unskilfully? Is it in accordance with my Buddha-nature? Could a *Buddha* behave in this way? Is it *possible*?' This 'Buddha-pride', as it is called, is a rather dangerous attitude for one to adopt. You could tell yourself, more modestly, not that you were a Buddha, but that you belong to the Buddha's spiritual family. You might say, 'How could I think of doing anything unskilful when I have been adopted into the family of the Buddha?' or even, 'I am a child of the Buddha; how could I disgrace my own father by behaving badly?'

Hand in hand with this kind of positive pride goes respect for the good qualities of others. In an earlier passage, Nāgārjuna has spoken of 'honouring the honourable', an expression which brings us up against a peculiarly modern wrong view. Today, the idea that one should reverence that which is worthy of reverence is rather foreign to us. People tend to be suspicious of anything which to them smacks of elitism. Since Freud, we have become very mistrustful of those who seem too good to be true, and we are only too aware that greatness may well conceal great weakness. Great achievements are often seen as compensations for the failure to address a deep emotional need. Along with this perception goes an urge to cut down to size anyone who succeeds in rising above the common herd. In the past, people were accustomed to look up to those in positions of social or political authority, in much the same way that they looked up to God. Now all that has gone. God is not worshipped as widely as before, and most people have completely lost the habit of looking up. Yet William Blake very truly observed that 'Worship of God is: honouring his gifts in other men each according to his genius, and loving the greatest men best'.[61] The same should go for us: if we really worship the Buddha, we will worship the spirit of his teaching wherever it manifests.

We are quick to expose hypocrisy, to ridicule solemnity, and to bring pomposity down to earth. We like to insist that our own opinions are no less valid than anyone else's. We pride ourselves on not toeing the party line, on sticking to our own point of view. It is difficult for us to appreciate how great a shift this represents from the attitude that prevailed until the middle of the twentieth century. People were then more prepared to set aside their own personal – and thus necessarily limited and partial – views and interests out of respect for the supposedly better informed judgements of those in authority. They took pride in 'doing their duty'. Nāgārjuna's 'honouring the honourable' could be rendered as 'respecting the respectable', and this shows us how alien such deference is to contemporary thinking.

But what are we left with if we refuse to look up to anyone, and if we are so satisfied with our present level of understanding that we cannot imagine anything surpassing it? In fact, human beings have a deep-seated need to worship, so that we will inevitably look for someone or something to meet that need. But sometimes we set up idols only to cast them down and trample upon them. Moreover, we remain in thrall to group evaluations, except that nowadays those evaluations are often devaluations. Our cynical assumption is that the more we know about people, the less we will find to respect. We assume that what we do not know must be discreditable. In fact, while some of what we do not know may indeed be discreditable, there is much that is good which, being beyond our ken, we are simply unable to appreciate. As Coleridge said, we can reverence only what we do not understand.[62]

One would have thought that people would prefer to look up, rather than to look down. But in cynicism there is more satisfaction for the ego, for we then feel that we know everything worth knowing about people and ideas and can reassure ourselves that no one is better than we are. We are capable of acknowledging someone's mastery in certain areas so long as we can shake our heads over their failings in others. Probably, it is the fear of seeming naive and gullible, as much as anything, that prevents us from looking up to anyone. The Buddhist approach is always to examine the mental state behind any attitude, and from this point of view, a knowing cynicism is no better than starry-eyed idolization.

To take the most obvious example of human greatness, that of the Buddha himself, do we revere him as a Buddha or do we see him as just one of us, as human and therefore flawed? Of course, he was a human being, but not just a human being. His being human does not make him less of a Buddha. Indeed, his humanity is part of his Buddhahood. It is not easy for us to see his humanity *and* his Enlightenment at the same time, but if we are able to do so, we will see him more truly and therefore reverence him more deeply. Likewise, while it does a disservice to the memory of any great individual to ignore the weaknesses that testify to their humanity, we do ourselves a disservice if we allow our knowledge of those weaknesses to blind us to the fact that their qualities are vastly superior to our own.

For a Buddhist, 'the honourable' means, primarily, the Three Jewels: the Buddha, the Dharma, and the Sangha. We honour the Enlightened human source of the Dharma, the Dharma or teaching itself, and those who communicate and exemplify the Dharma, that is, the noble Arhants and the glorious Bodhisattvas as well as those more developed individuals with whom we are in personal contact. Foremost among the latter is our own teacher. In Tibetan Buddhism, one's teacher is revered as the manifestation, within the mandala of the disciple's spiritual life, of the Buddha himself. This shows how far Tibetan Buddhists are prepared to go in their concern to protect people from the grave fault of failure to 'honour the honourable'.

IGNOBLE MOTIVES

Hypocrisy is to control the senses
For the sake of goods and respect.
Flattery is to speak pleasant phrases
For the sake of goods and respect.

Indirect acquisition is to praise
Another's wealth in order to acquire it.
Pressured acquisition is manifest derision
Of others in order to acquire goods.

Desiring profit from profit
Is to praise previous acquisitions.
Repeating faults is to recite again and again
The mistakes made by others.[63]

Here we have the opposite of failure to 'honour the honourable'. Hypocrisy and flattery are closely connected with concealment and dissimulation. An example of hypocrisy would be the adoption of the Buddhist lifestyle, whether as a monk in the East or as a Buddhist teacher in the West, for the sake of mundane rewards: an easy, pleasant life, respect, even quite a good living in some cases.

> I rather suspect that in the case of such Zen stories
> most people will identify with the wise master
> rather than with the ignorant disciple.

We flatter others not only 'for the sake of goods and respect', or to win their approval, but also out of fear. We are trying to placate them, to put them in a good frame of mind so as to render them less threatening. In India, flattery is often gross and open. People flatter you to your face in the most outrageous fashion, without the least hesitation or shame. I have been the object of embarrassing effusions of this kind myself when being introduced before delivering a talk. Some recipients of such flattery happily swallow it all, beaming down on the audience and nodding agreement and satisfaction with what is being said about them. This comes from their living in a hierarchical society in which flattery of superiors is regarded as right and proper. Here flattery is taken not so much as a statement of objective fact but rather as a clear indication of the recipient's importance and power and of the flatterer's dependence on that person's favour. In general, the Indian assumption seems to be that if you flatter someone sufficiently they can't refuse you anything that you ask.

A different kind of flattery comes into play when you cast your eye on a picture or some knick-knack, and say, 'I really do like that,' in such a way that the owner feels obliged to give it to you. Then there is the no less ignoble ploy of deprecating something for the same end: 'Oh, that doesn't really go with the rest of the decor, does it? It seems hardly worth keeping – it can't have cost you very much. *I* could find a home for it, though.' Another rather sordid tack Nāgārjuna warns us against is to tell someone how pleased you were with an object they gave you on some previous occasion, how useful it was, and how you could really do with another one just like it, in such a way that they too feel obliged to meet your wish. People have not changed much since Nāgārjuna's time.

An important Buddhist practice is to rejoice in the virtues of others, but unfortunately many of us prefer to dwell on their faults. ('Repeating faults is to recite again and again the mistakes made by others,' Nāgārjuna says.) But what are we really trying to achieve by doing that? Clearly we are looking down on the objects of our fault-finding in order to seem or feel superior by comparison. We try to distance ourselves from certain faults by criticizing them in others. A lot of humour works like this. The suggestion is that because we can see the folly or frailty of the person who is the butt of the joke and laugh at them, we are free from that folly ourselves. Laughter is sometimes accompanied by a feeling of relief – the relief that comes with recognizing a problem and knowing that one is not caught up in it oneself. The wide appeal of certain Zen stories, in which a stupid monk is shown up – and sometimes woken up – by a wise Zen master, is no doubt related to this human tendency to laugh at the stupidity of others. In a story, we inevitably identify at some level with one of the characters, and I rather suspect that in the case of such Zen stories most people will identify with the wise master rather than with the ignorant disciple.

PRIDE

Through arrogance, a bad lineage,
Through jealousy, little beauty.

A bad colour comes through anger,
Stupidity, from not questioning the wise.[64]

If you are arrogant you will eventually be looked down upon. This is the traditional Buddhist view. If you take pride in the eminence of your family or clan – or in modern terms, in your status as a professional – the result under the law of karma and rebirth is that you will be reborn in a low-class family and with low prospects. Jockeying for position is a natural and quite healthy feature of any human – indeed any animal – group. It is the way in which those who are stronger, cleverer, or more capable are enabled to influence the group as a whole. Within a healthy society, those who lack natural abilities at least understand the advantage of their relying for leadership on those who are better qualified. The ego exploits this kind of situation. When someone identifies with the status attached to a position of influence, that ego-identification will often find expression in arrogance, in which case they are probably less clever and capable than they think, because arrogance in the long run limits a person's ability to influence others. Arrogance is a presumption of higher status that depends upon treating others as inferior. But if you try to lord it over others, they will resent it and try to turn the tables on you. They might even succeed.

Sometimes, what appears to be arrogance is not really such, but is a wrong impression due to a misunderstanding or a clash of personalities. For example, within institutions there is often conflict between those individuals who are more highly organized and those who are less so. The first type will accuse the second of being lazy and unmotivated, while the latter will complain that the more highly organized are forever telling them what to do. This lack of understanding between the two types often manifests as the less organized perceiving the more organized as arrogant. But if you are truly cleverer or more capable you will try to appreciate ordinary people for what they are able to contribute, rather than looking down on them in a spirit of superiority.

JEALOUSY

Emotions like anger and jealousy also have consequences in terms of our outward appearance. If we are habitually jealous we begin to look sour, bitter, and resentful. Shakespeare makes Nāgārjuna's point better than anyone, when in *Othello* he has Iago express his jealousy of Cassio:

He hath a daily beauty in his life
That makes me ugly;

Jealousy is, in a way, the opposite of arrogance. One is the ego looking down, the other is the ego looking up. It is jealousy that makes us unwilling to rejoice in or even to acknowledge the success, the beauty, or the goodness of other people. We resent others for possessing qualities which, we feel, we do not possess. In fact it is jealousy that, by its very nature, makes it difficult for us to cultivate those qualities ourselves. In the *Bodhicaryāvatāra*, Śāntideva brings out the sheer irrationality of jealousy. Addressing the would-be Bodhisattva, he says, 'You desire Buddhahood ... expressly for living beings. Why do you burn inside on seeing them have some slight honour?'[65]

ANGER

Traditionally, one of the karmic consequences of anger, as of jealousy, is ugliness. Anger tends to distort the features, as one sees in many Renaissance drawings of grotesque faces.

Ageing, also, allows our character to find its way into our appearance; our predominant emotions leave their imprint on the face more and more deeply as we grow older. Oscar Wilde's story, *The Picture of Dorian Gray*, turns on this fact. A handsome young man keeps a portrait of himself in a locked room, and in a sinister and eerie reversal of the natural order of things, his portrait takes on the effects of ageing while he himself continues to look as young as when it was painted. Though he leads a thoroughly disreputable life, he does not appear to age at all. It is the portrait that slowly, day by day and year by year, shows the terrible consequences of his depravity in its painted features.

THE MANY FACES OF ATTACHMENT

Non-collectedness is inconsiderate irritation
Arisen from illness.
Clinging is the attachment
Of the lazy to their bad possessions.

Discrimination of differences is discrimination
Impeded by desire, hatred, or obscuration.
Not looking into the mind is explained
As not applying it to anything.

Degeneration of respect and reverence for deeds
Concordant with the practices occurs through laziness.
A bad person is regarded as being a spiritual guide
(Pretending) to have the ways of the Supramundane Victor.

Yearning is a small entanglement
Arising from lustful desire.
Obsession, a great entanglement
Arising from desire.

Avarice is an attitude
Of clinging to one's own property,
Inopportune avarice is attachment
To the property of others.

Irreligious lust is the desirous praise
Of women who ought to be avoided.
Hypocrisy is to pretend that one possesses
Good qualities that one lacks, while desiring ill deeds.

Great desire is extreme greed
Gone beyond the fortune of knowing satisfaction.
Desire for advantage is to want to be known
By whatever way as having superior good qualities.[66]

'Discrimination of differences' suggests that discrimination is of two kinds. Discrimination can be a positive thing, but seeing differences on the basis of desire, hatred, or obscuration is not. We interpret almost all of our perceptions through conditioned emotional responses that make distinctions where none really exist. It isn't wrong to discriminate, but that discrimination must be, as it were, objective. It must be a seeing of things as they really are. Objective discrimination is in fact a very positive quality. At the highest level it is one of the five wisdoms of the five-Buddha mandala: the discriminating wisdom of Amitābha, the *pratyavekṣaṇa jñāna*, which sees the uniqueness of things, and discriminates them from one another accordingly.

> We cannot see things as they really are
> so long as we are attached to them.

'Non-collectedness' in the first verse here means unmindfulness, and this is a fault that gives rise to a multitude of further faults. Becoming irritable when you are ill is one of them. Non-collectedness also means being scattered and prone to a mindless inconsiderate hilarity. One aspect of mindfulness is 'looking into the mind', which is achieved at least partly through applying the mind to a single object, and in this way unifying or integrating one's mental energies. This concentration or harmonization of the mind is the result of a process of weeding out unskilful mental states and developing skilful ones. By looking into the mind we make it still and calm, and by making it still and calm we are enabled to look more deeply into it. Thus the process goes on.

The first thing that most of us notice when we look into the mind is 'attachment' or 'entanglement', and on looking more deeply we find that this comes from simple human desires, desires arising out of the perception of certain objects. Attachment arises when we become emotionally dependent on the enjoyment of such objects. Thus desire comes first, leading to a smaller or a greater degree of entanglement, as the case may be. One becomes habituated to the enjoyment of a particular thing, and attachment therefore follows.

Really addictive or obsessive entanglements are obviously a problem, even from the mundane point of view, but they are not always spiritually the most dangerous. For a practising Buddhist, there is real danger in small entanglements. It is when we say, 'This little fault is not really important in the larger context of my practice,' that we need to be on our guard. It is like when one is weeding the garden and it seems too much trouble to dig out a bramble root. It looks harmless when there is only a small shoot, but before one knows it the garden is overgrown with brambles. In a way there is no such thing as a small fault, particularly if we do not deal with it straight away, any more than there is any such thing as a small weed. Dismissing 'small entanglements' amounts to not acknowledging the truly enormous obstacle standing between you and what is supposedly your goal. This obstacle is your unwillingness to clear away even quite small entanglements. The *Dhammapada* puts this well: 'Do not underestimate evil, thinking, "It will not approach me." A water-pot becomes full by the constant falling of drops of water. Similarly, the spiritually immature person little by little fills himself with evil.'[67]

The opposite attitude is considering as important things that really do not matter very much. Minor regulations become a substitute for spiritual principles. I have known Sri Lankan monks who were notorious for their strict observance of rules that most monks considered relatively unimportant, and who made a nuisance of themselves by insisting on following them to the letter. I remember a lunch held in the library of the Maha Bodhi Society headquarters in Calcutta in 1956, for which perhaps thirty or forty monks, mostly from Ceylon (as it was then), but also from Burma, Thailand, and other countries, had turned up. The food did not arrive until 11:40, so there was time to finish by twelve if you ate rather quickly. One of the monks present was known for his punctilious observance of the *Vinaya*, one of whose minor rules was not to take solid food after midday. He was shovelling food into his mouth as fast as he could, all the time watching the clock on the library wall as its hand crept towards the hour. The moment it struck twelve he dropped his spoon as though it was red hot, and looked round as though expecting everyone else to do likewise. But the rest of the monks took no notice of the clock and went on steadily eating, while he surveyed the scene with a very virtuous expression. As he left the room some of the senior monks just looked at each other and smiled, before returning to their meal.

Our most obvious attachments are to material things. What Nāgārjuna calls avarice is attachment to our own property – a particular shirt, say, or a special chair, or even a house. Similarly, inopportune avarice is attachment to the property of others. We all have a tendency to hang on to things, whether it is a book we have borrowed, or a book of our own that we are never going to read but which we keep anyway. It might seem that these attachments have little to do with our capacity to see into the nature of things, but in fact they represent our basic resistance to the truth. We cannot see things as they really are so long as we are attached to them.

Nāgārjuna has spoken of sexual attachment more than once. Here he warns against 'desirous praise of women who ought to be avoided'. We all know what this means. Such praise is

163

often a topic of masculine conversation, as well as being the staple of much commercial advertising. It comes from not seeing women as they really are, either in the more metaphysical sense, or even in simply human terms. 'Avoiding' women might seem an extreme measure but what it really means is just leaving them alone. I have talked to women about their experience of women's retreats, and they have often said that they found it a great relief to be 'left alone' in this way. They said that normally they did rather enjoy having men around, who gave them attention, and who perhaps even competed with one another for them. But in same-sex situations they nevertheless felt a sense of relief, as though a weight had been lifted from them.

Attachments occur in every connection, and we can be hypocritical when they clash. For example, we are attached to our faults, but we are also attached to our reputation, as Nāgārjuna has already pointed out. In Sanskrit and Tibetan there are several words that have to be rendered by the one English word 'hypocrisy', but here hypocrisy is the precise equivalent that is needed. It means being a 'whited sepulchre', pretending to be pure and holy while your heart is set on worldly things. The archetypal hypocrite is Tartuffe, the eponymous hero of Molière's famous comedy, from whom derives the word 'Tartuffery' (rarely used these days) for consummate hypocrisy in general.

The kind of attachment that can never be satisfied is represented by the *pretas* or hungry ghosts. Their neurotic craving is so intense that it is beyond even the possibility of satisfaction. This is the world of drug addiction or intense emotional dependency. Then there is the attachment we have to our own image or wanting 'to be known by whatever way as having superior good qualities'. The words 'by whatever way' make it clear why this kind of attachment involves such hard work. We want to be permanently identified with our own ideal image of ourselves, an image which we feel obliged to protect at all costs. Adulation can be a problem for the practising Buddhist, because the good qualities he or she has developed may end up becoming a cause for complacency and pride on their part.

Moral crusaders are like this. They are the holier-than-thou castigators of people's moral shortcomings. In some cases, no doubt, their sense of outrage is justified, but one suspects that many of them are just trying to attract attention to themselves and to make others feel uncomfortable. Some vegetarians, for example, do this to the unfortunate meat-eater. However worthy their work may be, it is the vehemence with which single-issue activists insist on the unique importance of their particular cause that often makes their position suspect. In India I once met a man, to take another example, who thought that everybody with a social conscience should be helping the lepers, just as he was doing. If you were not doing that, you were morally bankrupt. By identifying strongly with one worthwhile cause, you put yourself in a superior moral position. You create a situation in which you are one of the few who are in the right, which enables you to look down on everyone else. The more importance you give to your cause, the more importance you give to yourself.

HIDDEN INTENTIONS

Attachment to objects is to relate
Their good qualities in order to acquire them.
Fancying immortality is to be
Unaffected by concern over death.

Conceptuality concerned with approbation
Is the thought that – no matter what –
Others will take one as a spiritual guide
Due to possessing good qualities.

Conceptuality concerned with attachment to others
Is an intention to help or not help others

Due to being affected by desire
Or an intent to harm.[68]

Here Nāgārjuna exposes quite a varied collection of human vanities and attachments. 'Fancying immortality' is falsely believing that you will go marching on after death just as you are, that you will survive death more or less intact. This is a form of eternalism, or the over-literal view of rebirth: the idea that you will just wake up on the other side almost exactly as you are on this side, either to be reborn straightaway or to select a rebirth at your leisure, or else to spend a few hundred years in some pleasant heavenly realm.

> The fact is that we cannot delay
> embarking on compassionate action
> until such time as our motive is completely pure.

This is a deluded view, to put it mildly. No doubt we ought to be concerned about death, which can be a traumatic experience. Most of us are very attached to the things of this world, whether we like to admit it or not, and we are going to suffer when we are torn away from them. So we should be concerned about death, and about what will happen to us afterwards. We certainly should not imagine that death will necessarily be simply a smooth transition to some other state.

The second verse quoted here refers to the way we casually let drop hints as to our social status when we meet people. There might not be any conscious intention to establish ourselves as superior; we drop such hints almost automatically. In India people often ask one's caste (or at least they used to), in order to find out where they stand in relation to you. In the West it is often our job that is the key indicator of our social status. Either way, we feel we need to know these things and we feel the need to communicate the more favourable indicators of our own status in order to secure as high a place in the social pecking order as we can. Some people do this to a ridiculous degree: 'My neighbour in Cannes was so late getting from his estate to the film studios that he had to borrow my helicopter.' Or, more subtly, 'Of course, my last book didn't do all that well, you know.' This tendency can easily find its way into the religious sphere, even into the sangha, which is presumably the context Nāgārjuna has in mind. People say, 'You wouldn't believe how damp my cave in the Himalayas was,' or 'A funny thing happened on my second three-year meditation retreat,' or even, 'As the Dalai Lama said to me, the last time we met,...' The hidden intention here is to assert one's spiritual prestige and status. In saying such things we are not necessarily laying claim to any actual spiritual attainment. We are not openly claiming anything at all. But hints of this kind are worse, in a way, than open bragging.

The next verse uncovers more hidden motives. However, being aware of these is no reason for us to condemn ourselves on their account. Our good intentions are often not entirely pure. We may even get a kick out of being altruistic. We are not in it just to help others; we enjoy being in the position of being the helper, the one others look up to. This is only natural. It is very difficult to be entirely disinterested in one's efforts to help others. There is almost always something in it for us, even if it is only that we accumulate merit or go to heaven when we die.

The fact is that we cannot delay embarking on compassionate action until such time as our motive is completely pure. We have to work on our motivation at the same time that we are engaged in such action. The real danger is that we might be getting out of our altruism some satisfaction that we do not acknowledge. But if we bring mindfulness to bear on our motives it will help purify them. In the early days of the Western Buddhist Order, people sometimes told me that they did not want to ask for ordination until they could be sure that their motive was perfectly pure. I used to say, 'In that case, you'll wait for ever. Your motives will never be completely pure. Your motives for committing yourself to the Buddhist path will always be tainted with self-interest. It's enough if on balance you feel that your motive is predominately pure.' Our Going for Refuge becomes complete only with Enlightenment, but in the meantime the very fact that we go for Refuge has the effect of helping to purify the motive with which we go for Refuge.

It is the same with meditation. You do not learn all about meditation before you start meditating. You learn a little, and then later, in the light of some practical experience, you correct or modify the ideas that led you to take it up. And so the process goes on. The reasons for which people stay with something, whether it is meditation, Buddhism, or a particular spiritual community (or even a marriage) are sometimes quite different from those with which they began. We are adjusting our direction, or our vision, or our motive, all the time.

MENTAL STATES HAVE CONSEQUENCES

Dislike is a mind that is unsteady,
Desiring union is a dirtied mind.
Indifference is a laziness with a sense of inadequacy
Coming from a listless body.

Distortion is for the afflictive emotions
To influence body and colour.
Not wishing for food is explained
As physical sluggishness due to over-eating.

A very dejected mind is taught
To be fearful faintheartedness.
Longing for desires is to desire
And to seek after the five attributes.[69]

Harmful intent arises from nine causes
Of intending to injure others –
Having senseless qualms concerning oneself, friends, and foes
In the past, present, and future.

Sluggishness is non-activity
Due to heaviness of mind and body.
Drowsiness is sleepiness.
Excitement is strong disquiet of body and mind.

Contrition is regret for bad deeds
Which arises afterwards from grief about them.
Doubt is to be of two minds
About the (four) truths, the Three Jewels, and so forth.

(Householder) Bodhisattvas abandon those.
Those diligent in (monastic) vows abandon more.
Freed from these defects
Good qualities are easily observed.

Briefly the good qualities
Observed by Bodhisattvas are
Giving, ethics, patience, effort,
Concentration, wisdom, compassion, and so forth.

Giving is to give away one's wealth.
Ethics is to help others.
Patience is to have forsaken anger.
Effort is enthusiasm for virtues.

Concentration is unafflicted one-pointedness.
Wisdom is ascertainment of the meaning of the truths.
Compassion is a mind having one savour
Of mercy for all sentient beings.

From giving there arises wealth, from ethics happiness,
From patience a good appearance, from (effort in) virtue brilliance,
From concentration peace, from wisdom liberation,
From compassion all aims are achieved.

From the simultaneous perfection
Of all those seven is attained
The sphere of inconceivable wisdom,
The protectorship of the world.[70]

Negative mental states do not simply pass through the mind leaving no trace behind; they have an effect on us. The mind becomes sullied or stirred up or dull and inert, and this unsatisfactory state of affairs tends to produce further negative mental states. Timidity saps our energy, our confidence, our strength. Eating too much makes us physically and mentally sluggish. All these negative states can also affect the health and general appearance of the body. They are felt in the body, and if they are habitual the body begins to register them in terms of posture or facial expression, and even in terms of the blood pressure.

Note that Nāgārjuna recommends that we should never eat so much that our appetite is fully satisfied. Healthy desire, such as the desire for food or for exercise, is positive; the energy in it is necessary for developing a powerful aspiration towards Enlightenment. Desire is unhelpful only to the extent that it is caught up in sense-objects. Aversion, too, can be useful, especially when it is directed towards *saṃsāra*. But generally our aversion takes the form of hatred or 'harmful intent', which arises from 'senseless qualms', i.e. from baseless fears, anxieties, and insecurities which in some cases may amount to paranoia.

Contrition is usually reckoned as a positive quality, but here it means the regret that is experienced when one's bad deeds produce unpleasant consequences one had not foreseen. You are not sorry that you have behaved unskilfully; you feel sorry because your bad deeds have not proved successful or have got you into trouble, leaving you with a bad reputation.

If you are 'of two minds' about such things as the Four Noble Truths or the Three Jewels,[71] this is because you are unintegrated. The idiom 'to be of two minds' is revealing. It acknowledges that you can have, as it were, two minds that operate at one and the same time, or at least that jostle each other for control of your life. Faith, by contrast, implies that you are integrated, that you are of the same mind about such things as the Four Noble Truths and the Three Jewels from one moment to the next. You retain a clear and conscious belief in the values they represent, and it is these values that give you your identity as a Buddhist.

Faith is to be distinguished from blind faith. Faith does not exclude honest doubt in the sense of openness of mind or suspension of belief until such time as one has sufficient grounds for making up one's mind. But doubt as a fault does not consist in just being of two minds. It is not really wanting to know what one thinks, and therefore not making a genuine effort to find out. The reason we are so loath to pursue the truth is simple. It is because once we have ascertained it, we might have to take up a definite attitude towards it, or do something about it, or even commit ourselves to its realization.

The faults enumerated by Nāgārjuna are to be abandoned by both monk and householder. As far as the Bodhisattva path is concerned, the Buddhist householder is expected to work on the elimination of all these negative tendencies in the same way that the monk is, though the monk has other precepts to observe in addition. Nāgārjuna is on safe ground when he assures the king that if he takes care of these defects, the corresponding virtues will take care of themselves. The virtues are the opposite of the faults. Once again, though, we must question the practical usefulness of presenting the spiritual life in predominantly negative terms. We have to assume that while the faults themselves are negative, the ancient Indians had the capacity to engage with them in a positive manner. For us, it is surely better to think in terms of cultivating fifty-seven virtues than correcting fifty-seven faults.

7

THE RESULTS OF ACTIONS

Throughout the *Precious Garland*, Nāgārjuna takes it for granted, as does the whole of the Buddhist tradition, that the law of karma operates not just within our lifetime, but over a series of lives. The advantage of this belief is that it helps to make sense of our observation that some people seem to 'get away with' committing unskilful actions. However, it may be more useful to consider the very real consequences of our actions in this life, regardless of whatever retribution may or may not be waiting for us in our next. What we do and what we experience as a result are directly connected here and now, not just that actions are matched with 'just deserts', but that the results of actions are part and parcel of the actions themselves. There is no cosmic policeman handing out speeding tickets. It is our own actions that help create our character.

Buddhist ethics are bound up with motivation. It is the intention behind your actions that constitutes karma, rather than the actions as such. Of course, if the intention expresses itself in action, the karma will be much more powerful than it would be if you simply imagined yourself doing something skilful or unskilful. At the same time, if you happen to do something accidentally, the relevant karma will pertain to the lack of mindfulness – or perhaps the intoxication – that was responsible for the accident, and this lack of mindfulness is bound up with motivation.

A short life comes through killing.
Much suffering comes through harming.
Poor resources, through stealing.
Enemies, through adultery.[72]

Here Nāgārjuna speaks about the consequences of specific actions, i.e. those relating to the breaking of the first three of the ten precepts. But how does the act of intentional killing shorten one's life? If you create around yourself an atmosphere of anger, hatred, and fear, you are likely to attract those people for whom that kind of atmosphere is natural, and who are at home in it. Acts of extreme violence require a very powerful charge of ill will. When you kill, you are 'tuning in' to a particular wavelength or to a particular realm of being. You will then tend to find yourself in the same world as other people who are inclined to kill, and of course it is quite likely that you will be the victim of one of them at some point. Alternatively, it may be guilt on account of what you have done that draws you into situations in which you, in your turn, may be harmed and thus punished.

> To identify the kind of suffering
> that must follow an unskilful action,
> one has only to look at the mentality behind the action.

This kind of approach, though not the traditional one, has the advantage of reflecting the complexity of the karmic process. One could easily jump to the conclusion that if someone dies young, for example, it is because they killed someone in a previous life. But this does not necessarily follow. There are a number of reasons, other than karma, for a person's early demise. The fact that actions have consequences does not mean that everything that happens to one is the karmic result of actions one has committed in this or in previous lives. This applies to all the examples of unskilful actions and their consequences given by Nāgārjuna.

Generally speaking, those who harm living beings will suffer. But do they always suffer in this life? Obviously not, it has to be said. Certainly they suffer no more than do many who are clearly innocent. Likewise, many who steal acquire considerable wealth, especially those who steal by devious means, like crooked financiers. But harming others is always dangerous. You will inevitably create animosity in those you harm, and sooner or later that animosity will be directed against you. It is significant that fierce competition is sometimes referred to as 'cut-throat' competition, and if you cut the throat of your competitor, you must expect that he will try to cut yours.

To identify the kind of suffering that must follow an unskilful action, one has only to look at the mentality behind the action. One has to imagine the mental state of one who is bent on harming others to know the kind of suffering they will eventually have to experience. As for stealing, this is the expression of a mind that is never satisfied with what it has. If killing is natural to the beings in hell, stealing is natural to the *pretas*, or 'hungry ghosts'. *Preta*-like people are always on the lookout for what they can appropriate. This is no less true of petty thieves than it is of crooked multimillionaires. So driven are they by acquisitiveness that they lose the capacity to appreciate and enjoy what they possess, as well as losing their ability to appreciate people. Human relationships are trampled underfoot in the pursuit of profit.

According to Nāgārjuna, the result of adultery is that one makes enemies. Adultery is not just a matter of stealing another person's spouse; one is seriously disrupting that person's whole life. It may be one thing to break up a casual sexual relationship, particularly when one is young, but it is quite another to break up a long-standing marriage, especially when there are children. You will probably deeply offend two entire families. In ancient times an adulterous affair could set off a feud that lasted for generations. If we are to believe Homer, the adultery of Paris with Helen of Troy led to a ten-year war that resulted in the destruction of an ancient city and the loss of thousands of lives.

These are effects for humans,
But prior to all is a bad transmigration.[73]

We have been discussing all these faults with respect to the impact they have in the present life, and it is clear that within the span of one lifetime their consequences can be disastrous. But it is worth bearing in mind that for Nāgārjuna, as for most Buddhists throughout history, their *principal* 'fruit' is a bad rebirth.

THE FRUITS OF VIRTUE

Opposite to the well-known
Fruits of these non-virtues
Is the arising of effects
Caused by all the virtues.

Desire, hatred, ignorance, and
The actions they generate are non-virtues.
Non-desire, non-hatred, non-ignorance,
And the actions they generate are virtues.[74]

It might seem odd that the beneficial fruits of skilful actions should be couched in negative terms in certain respects. It is almost as though the moral virtues had no character of their own but consisted simply in not acting unskilfully. The implication is that the negative is, as it were, the original position and the positive merely the negation of the negative. But these negative terms are not really as negative as they seem. In Sanskrit, the words *alobha*, *adveṣa*, and *amoha* are formed by adding the negative prefix a- to the terms *lobha* (desire), *dveṣa* (hatred), and *moha* (ignorance), but in each case the connotation is not negative but positive. We find the same thing in the case of English. Terms like 'immortal', 'infinite', and 'immaculate' have a much more positive meaning than their negative form might suggest. Though formally they are negations of other terms, they stand as positive terms in their own right. Many Sanskrit and Pāli negative terms work in a similar way. They may be grammatically negative, but the impression they convey is often more positive than a literal English translation is able to communicate. That language appears to falter before these positive qualities, or these ideas, suggests that they are really beyond conceptual understanding.

> If, in teaching the Dharma,
> we have occasion to tell people
> what it is *not* good for them to do,
> we should make sure that we also tell them,
> in the same breath if possible,
> what it *is* good for them to do.

However, does the fact that language is inadequate mean that we have to start from our experience of the morally negative? It is true that most people are caught up in all sorts of negative mental states and unskilful habits which, to begin with, have to be given up. But what is going to inspire us to give them up? It will surely be something positive. And how can that positive quality inspire us if it is simply the negation of something negative? There is nothing particularly Dharmic about expressing positive qualities by giving negative prefixes to negative terms. It is purely a matter of Indian linguistic and literary convention. Indeed, a positive term such as the Sanskrit *maitrī* (*mettā* in Pāli) is more truly positive than any of its negatively-formed equivalents.

Nāgārjuna spells out the negative consequences of various unskilful actions of body, speech, and mind and then adds, almost as an afterthought, that the corresponding skilful actions will have correspondingly positive results. He could have presented things in the opposite way, spelling out the positive results of skilful actions and leaving us to work out the negative consequences of unskilful actions for ourselves. That he does not do so is just a matter of Indian linguistic convention; it has nothing to do with the Dharma as such. Putting things negatively may have worked in the past, but in the modern context it is probably better to think of the moral virtues in more positive and inspiring terms, and to dwell on the positive results of skilful actions, rather than on the negative consequences of unskilful ones. Otherwise, we may give people the impression that the Dharma is just the taking away of something, and its goal a mere absence.

This is a common misconception of Buddhism, especially in the West. In the popular imagination, *nirvāṇa* is often a literal snuffing out, and *śūnyatā* literally a yawning void, a blank emptiness.[75] It is as though one disappeared over the edge of Enlightenment into complete nothingness. In view of this understandable but utterly mistaken reading of the Dharma, we should be careful that we do not, as a matter of course, couch its supremely positive ideals in negative terms. Certainly in English at least, negative terms do not do justice to the sublime union of wisdom and compassion, which is the ultimate goal of the spiritual life. If, in teaching the Dharma, we have occasion to tell people what it is *not* good for them to do, we should make sure that we also tell them, in the same breath if possible, what it *is* good for them to do.

DEVELOPING A NEW WORLD

Through multitudes of pure wishes
Your Buddha Land will be purified.

Through offering gems to the King of Subduers
You will emit infinite light.

Therefore knowing the concordance
Of actions and their effects,
Always help beings in fact.
Just that will help yourself.[76]

The advice here is simple: we should make sure our actions accord with the effects we want to produce. We know that the best way of helping ourselves is to help others. Of course we often forget and revert to acting as if it were otherwise. So how do we remind ourselves? The easiest way, perhaps, is to rely on regular contact with spiritual friends, whose advice and example will jog our memory.

> The principle underlying the myth
> is that of the power of positive thinking.

The Sanskrit term for Buddha Land is *buddhakṣetra*, and the idea of such a realm is based on the principle that thoughts can give rise to things, and that spiritual aspiration can be a creative force. For instance, if you practise generosity, if you have a generous heart, then, under the law of karma, you will be well provided for materially in the future. That is, we live in a certain kind of world, a world with certain general characteristics that give us a certain kind of experience. This world, this particular realm of experience, has been created by our actions. Our 'collective karma' produces the world in which we collectively live.

By changing your karma, however – that is, changing your mental state, your volitions or aspirations – you can modify your future environment. From this simple law can be extrapolated the further possibility that if your volitions or aspirations are sufficiently powerful, you will be able to create a whole world of your own, a world better and purer than worlds usually are.

Pure Buddha Lands feature prominently in the Mahāyāna scriptures. They are depicted as the ideal environment in which to practise the Dharma and are often described in lavish detail. Each one is produced by a particular Buddha, not with a view to his living in it in solitary splendour, but so that others might be reborn in it and practise the Dharma under his guidance more easily than they could in an ordinary, impure world. His Pure Land is the product of his intense and sustained aspiration, as a Bodhisattva, to bring such a world into existence. It is pure in the sense that it is inhabited only by human beings and gods. In it there are no animals, no asuras, no pretas, and no hell-beings. Moreover, there is no distinction of gender. One does not need to work, food and clothing appear spontaneously, and one is free to listen to the Dharma day and night.

The idea of the Buddha Land or Buddhafield need not be taken literally. It is myth, especially when named Buddhas are represented as creating their individual Buddhafields. The principle underlying the myth is that of the power of positive thinking, as it used to be called. If you think positively, if you radiate positive emotion, especially the more refined spiritual emotions, you will have a subtle but perceptible effect on your surroundings; you will create a positive atmosphere, almost like an aura or a magnetic field, that influences everyone within its compass.

Any powerful personality tends to create around them a world that reflects their character and values. Some people set up an inharmonious world; others, one that is intensely fearful or suspicious. Politicians tend to create asura-like worlds of ruthless ambition, while artists tend to create worlds dedicated to beauty and other aesthetic values. In the case of a Buddha, his wisdom and compassion create a 'gravitational field' so strong that it affects all who come within its range. This is his world, his Buddhafield.

In certain Mahāyāna sutras, this kind of phenomenon is vastly extended and amplified. They hold that a Buddha can, by sheer power of thought, create a whole ideal realm within which other living beings may be reborn. And there is more than a simple difference of degree between a Pure Buddhafield and an ordinary, impure Buddhafield, because the former is a separate, ideal environment, distinct from our own world. It has been brought into existence by an individual Bodhisattva's unaided efforts, by means of his or her own entirely pure thoughts, aspirations, and vows. An impure Buddhafield, by contrast, overlaps with the ordinary world. The Buddha shares it with other beings who have brought that world into existence by virtue of their impure karma.

It is like the difference between trying to practise the Dharma in the midst of ordinary city life, with all its distractions and difficulties, and doing so in a rural retreat centre. Such a centre is a small temporary Pure Land, where spiritually positive external conditions have been deliberately created. Its sole purpose is to enable retreatants to hear and practise the Dharma.

According to the Mahāyāna, the way to ensure rebirth in a Pure Land is to make a solemn aspiration to be reborn in one, and then to engage in the appropriate spiritual practice. The best known of these Pure Lands or Pure Buddhafields is Sukhāvatī, or 'abounding in bliss', the Pure Land of Amitābha, the Buddha of Infinite Light. This Pure Land figures prominently in Far Eastern Buddhism, where it is a central feature of the various Pure Land schools of China and Japan. These schools emphasize the importance of paying homage to Amitābha or chanting his name.

This Pure Land form of Buddhism seems to have arisen out of a widespread sense of spiritual despair. People felt it was no longer possible for them to attain Enlightenment in this world, where conditions were so unfavourable to the practice of the Dharma. They therefore aspired to be reborn not in this impure world but in a completely different world where conditions for practice were ideal. The Vajrayāna saw things differently. This world itself is the Pure Land, could we only see it as such. As you become pure yourself, the world too becomes pure or, rather, you experience it as pure. You are living in the midst of a divine mandala, not just in this defiled old world. You hear all sounds as mantras, see all forms as those of Buddhas and Bodhisattvas. Thus the Vajrayāna comes back to the general principle underlying the myth of the Pure Land, namely that we create our own worlds, whether now or in the future.

You can change the realm in which you live by setting up the conditions that will support a positive change in your mental states. In fact you are creating a world of your own around you all the time. The question is, what sort of world are you creating? And how are you going about creating it? A lot depends upon the kind of people with whom you associate, who will either draw you up to their own level of existence or drag you down. A Buddhist centre, for example, should be a little world, or at least an oasis, of awareness and kindness, quite different from other social environments. When one enters, it should look different, feel different, and be different, otherwise it isn't really a Buddhist centre at all. One should feel drawn into a lighter, purer, deeper realm of being.

Just as it is explained in medicine
That poison can be removed by poison,
What contradiction is there in saying
That what is injurious (in the future) can be removed by suffering?

It is renowned (in Great Vehicle scriptures) that motivation
*   determines practices*
And that the mind is most important.

Hence how could even suffering not be helpful
For one who gives help with an altruistic motivation?

If even (in ordinary life) pain can bring future benefit,
What need is there to say that (accepting suffering)
Beneficial for one's own and others' happiness will help!
This practice is known as the policy of the ancients.

If through relinquishing small pleasures
There is extensive happiness later,
Seeing the greater happiness
The resolute should relinquish small pleasures.

If such things cannot be borne,
Then doctors giving distasteful medicines
Would disappear. It is not (reasonable)
To forsake (great pleasure for the small).

Sometimes what is thought harmful
Is regarded as helpful by the wise.
General rules and their exceptions
Are commended in all treatises.[77]

We are all prepared, in certain circumstances, to endure a little pain in order to avoid a greater suffering later on. Yet for the sake of our little mundane pleasures we deny ourselves the far deeper pleasure, happiness, and fulfilment of the spiritual life. If someone in whom you have absolute trust were to say, 'Give me ten pounds today and I'll give you a hundred pounds tomorrow,' and you were to refuse the offer, you would in fact be refusing to give up ten pounds while being perfectly willing to give up a hundred pounds. It just makes no sense! Similarly, it makes no sense if one would rather forfeit the bliss of *nirvāṇa* than give up the pleasures of worldly life.

All this sounds very logical, but whether we act in accordance with it depends upon our having faith. We need to be deeply convinced of the rewards ultimately in store for us before giving up those right under our nose. A bird in the hand, as they say, is worth two in the bush. Most people's attitude will be, 'Give me a clear and compelling *experience* of the rewards of the spiritual life, and no doubt my interest in mundane pleasures will drop away quite naturally.' But in order to enjoy spiritual pleasures you have to give up worldly pleasures at least to some extent, and to do this you need to be resolute and determined. People find it difficult to give up habits like smoking, despite the clear health benefits of doing so. It is going to be much more difficult to give things up for the sake of less tangible benefits.

> The person who wears the shoe knows where it pinches.

Moreover, the spiritual rewards in store are not really to be compared with mundane rewards. We might have heard of spiritual pleasures, but I suspect that if one was to ask practitioners which were the greatest pleasures they had ever enjoyed, few would mention spiritual ones. They would probably come up with things like sex, drink, food, films, or perhaps music. The pleasures of meditation and the Dharma will seem to most of them rather anaemic in comparison. Spiritual pleasures may sometimes be very intense, but they are by nature a lot more subtle than are the pleasures of the senses. The idea of giving up worldly enjoyments for a few moments of meditative rapture every once in a while will seem to most people a poor bargain. Spiritual rewards are subtle and complex, being more a matter of fulfilment, peace, contentment, and freedom than simply a question of pleasure, however rarefied.

The argument suggests that pain or discomfort or deprivation is a safe investment, and I am not convinced that this is really the case. Nor does it express the true Bodhisattva spirit. We are being invited to practise the Dharma not because doing so is intrinsically attractive and inspiring but because it is a safer investment of our time and energy than any mundane option. It will pay better dividends and you will get a better return for

183

your money, so to speak. There is something less than elevating, even something ignoble, about such an argument.

Whatever the situation might have been in Nāgārjuna's time, today it is probably unwise glibly to advise people to give up the trivial, trashy pleasures of the world for the sake of the great spiritual pleasures to come, or to assure them that any sacrifice they make now will eventually prove to have been well worth it. To give up small pleasures in the hope of enjoying greater pleasures later on is something of a gamble. In any case, human beings need pleasure just to keep going. If life is devoid of pleasure of any kind, a reaction will surely kick in sooner or later; the denied need will make itself felt and in the end one is likely to resort to the grosser worldly pleasures rather than to the more refined ones in order to satisfy it.

Pleasure is an essential part of human life. Without it, the spiritual life itself becomes so joyless, dull, and arid that the practitioner may eventually lose interest in it altogether. The secret is to make sure that such pleasure is not incompatible with the spiritual life. Pleasurable experience that is skilful – and mundane pleasures *can* be skilful – has a tonic effect on the system. It is a mistake to imagine that by forcing ourselves to give up all our little pleasures now, we automatically move closer to the day when we will experience the pleasures of the spiritual life in all their glory. This is not necessarily so. It would be like setting off on a week's journey thinking that if you do not weigh yourself down with food you will get to your destination more quickly. Travelling light might serve your purpose for the first day or two, but after that you will slow right down, and may give up altogether due to lack of nourishment. Small pleasures should be enjoyed quite consciously, for the sake of one's overall spiritual progress, not indulged in or snatched at furtively or guiltily.

Worldly pleasures, being ultimately unreal and ultimately unsatisfying, are not to be relied on and may even be harmful. But engaging with your friends in innocent recreation that leaves you with more positive energy than you had before, can only be beneficial. Milarepa, the eleventh-century Tibetan poet and hermit, may have given up all worldly pleasures, but his songs are full of the joys of the spiritual life. We have to be honest about how much spiritual joy we actually experience, and must be careful to make up for what may be lacking in that respect with the help of relatively skilful mundane enjoyments. Otherwise we may experience a strong reaction against the spiritual life itself. On the other hand, we must be quite honest about the importance we give to pleasure, whether we 'go for refuge' to it, or are simply making room for it within the larger context of our lives as Buddhists.

The human attitude to pleasure and pain is a complex one. It may well be that those who are really struggling with difficulties will come out better and stronger in the end – but not necessarily. Nobody, however philosophical they may be, wants to lose all their money or to have their house burn down, and such calamities may even plunge some people into a prolonged depression. This important caveat aside, Nāgārjuna's point is crucial for the spiritual life. The wise person will always be able to turn a very real difficulty into an opportunity. Some people do not need to experience a hard time and may be very inspired, and fully committed to the spiritual life, without ever experiencing one. But for others, a hard time might be just what they need to bring about a radical change for the better in their life.

There are people who object to spiritual practice on the grounds that though it is supposed to free us from suffering, it nonetheless brings us varying degrees of discomfort, both physical and mental. Buddhist lifestyles seem to be all about the giving up of ordinary pleasures and comforts. However, any suffering experienced in the course of spiritual practice is only incidental. It is not the only result, nor even the necessary result of such practice. Solitary confinement is regarded by most people as a punishment. Naturally, therefore, they imagine that there is little joy to be had from a solitary retreat. 'Wouldn't you go mad with boredom?' they will say, 'Surely it's just masochism.' But the wise see solitude, when undertaken voluntarily, as a highly beneficial spiritual challenge. It may be difficult, even painful at times; one might experience boredom and even moments of despair, but if one persists, one will access inner resources that will be experienced as deeply enriching and pleasurable. Though sometimes painful, the process will eventually lead to blissful mental states and even to the bliss of liberation.

If your basic motivation is to help others, any pain that you experience in the course of making good this aspiration is going to enable you to be helpful in the long run. This can be quite a fruitful way of regarding any difficulties you may experience, especially when you are trying to follow the Bodhisattva path. Suffering is also helpful in a more direct way, in that it helps you to understand the suffering of others. If you haven't suffered much, you are less likely to be able to empathize with those who have. Again, this is not an absolute rule. If you have sufficient imagination, you need little pain of your own in order to empathize deeply with the pain of others. But if you have always enjoyed good health, for example, you might tend to think that people who are often ill and physically frail are making a lot of fuss about nothing, and should pull themselves together and stop complaining. Or, if you have never smoked, you can be quite unsympathetic towards those who feel the need for a cigarette twenty or thirty times a day: 'What do you mean, you can't give it up?' you say, 'All you need is a little will-power.'

This lack of sympathy, based on having too easy a life oneself, can extend into quite diverse areas. If you are full of faith, for example, you may be less than understanding towards someone who is racked by spiritual doubts. Or, if you are quite content with a celibate life, it can be hard for you to appreciate the difficulties and responsibilities of someone who is married and has a family. But those who have experienced problems in their personal life, or who have discovered their own human weakness, often become more sympathetic to others. Those who can remember their own early difficulties with meditation are often the best teachers of the subject. They certainly will not insist on long sessions of meditation for beginners, sessions that can only result in discomfort and boredom.

It is very difficult to enter into another person's experience. It is difficult for a law-abiding citizen to feel sympathy for the convicted criminal, or for the criminal to feel sympathy for the law-abiding citizen who helps to send him to jail. The person who wears the shoe knows where it pinches, as the proverb goes. When it comes to defining compassion, I fall back on Tennyson's phrase, 'some painless sympathy with pain'.[78] But the way to that state is generally found through a personal experience of pain, whether in the form of chronic illness, sudden bereavement, or crushing humiliation.

(The limitlessness of the merit of) wishing to help limitless realms
Of sentient beings is like (the limitlessness of those beings).

These practices that I have explained
Briefly to you in this way
Should be as dear to you
As your body always is.

Those who feel a dearness for the practices
Have in fact a dearness for their body.
If dearness (for the body) helps it,
The practices will do just that.

Therefore pay heed to the practices as you do to yourself.
Pay heed to achievement as you do to the practices.
Pay heed to wisdom as you do to achievement.
Pay heed to the wise as you do to wisdom.

Those who have qualms that it would be bad for themselves
(If they relied) on one who has purity, love, and intelligence

187

As well as helpful and appropriate speech,
Cause their own interests to be destroyed.

You should know in brief
The qualifications of spiritual guides.
If you are taught by those knowing contentment
And having compassion and ethics,

As well as wisdom that can drive out your afflictive emotions,
You should realize (what they teach) and respect them.
You will attain the supreme achievement
By following this excellent system:

Speak the truth, speak gently to sentient beings.
Be of pleasant nature, compelling.
Be politic, do not wish to defame,
Be independent, and speak well.

Be well-disciplined, contained, generous,
Magnificent, of peaceful mind,
Not excitable, not procrastinating,
Not deceitful, but amiable.

Be gentle like a full moon.
Be lustrous like the sun in autumn.
Be deep like the ocean.
Be firm like Mount Meru.

Freed from all defects
And adorned with all good qualities,
Become a sustenance for all sentient beings
And become omniscient.

These doctrines were not just taught
Only for monarchs,
But were taught with a wish to help
Other sentient beings as befits them.

O King, it would be right for you
Each day to think about this advice

So that you and others may achieve
Complete and perfect enlightenment.

For the sake of enlightenment aspirants should always
  apply themselves
To ethics, supreme respect for teachers, patience, non-jealousy,
  non-miserliness,
Endowment with the wealth of altruism without hope for reward,
  helping the destitute,
Remaining with supreme people, leaving the non-supreme,
  and thoroughly maintaining the doctrine.[79]

If the number of beings is limitless, then the merit accruing from wishing to help that limitless number of beings in limitless worlds is itself limitless. The practices that support this wish should therefore be valued accordingly. In the Indian idiom, they should be as dear to you as your own body or, as it is also said, your own eyes. The argument here is that one should look after one's spiritual practice with the same healthy attachment and daily attention to detail as one looks after one's body. You should feed, nourish, and cherish your practice as you do your body, to keep it alive and thriving. It is not something you can pick up and let drop when you feel like it. It has a life of its own, and it can die of neglect if one allows it to do so.

> We do not need to sit at the feet of a fully realized master;
> we need human contact....

Just as the body finds its highest purpose in acting as a support for spiritual practice, so the spiritual practice itself must have some higher purpose of its own. We should take care of our practice just as we do of our empirical self, especially the physical body. But it is not enough to practise mechanically. We should ask ourselves, 'Am I making any progress? What difference are the practices making? Am I eliminating the unskilful and developing the skilful?' It seems that for Nāgārjuna,

189

'achievement' means achievement in meditation, though even this is not enough in itself. You may be radiating friendliness, compassion, sympathetic joy, and equanimity, but wisdom ultimately lies beyond these. Meditational achievement is for the sake of attaining wisdom.

Surely, once one has attained to wisdom, there can be nothing further to which one needs to pay attention. Why, then, does Nāgārjuna go on to advise us to 'pay heed to the wise as you do to wisdom'? If you have wisdom yourself, surely there can be no need to pay heed to the wise? Nāgārjuna's point is that in a sense there is no such thing as wisdom. There are only wise individuals. 'Wisdom' is just an abstract term, but if you meet a wise person you do in fact encounter wisdom. You may fancy that you have developed wisdom, but you can know if you have really done so only by coming into contact with a wise person, and through the existential exchange that takes place between you and that particular human embodiment of wisdom. It is folly, as Nāgārjuna observes, to have reservations about one's reliance on such a teacher.

Wisdom is not an abstraction. It can exist only in living men and women. It has to be embodied. In fact, it is of the nature of wisdom to distinguish between concepts and lived experience. You may think you have it, but the real test is how you fare when you meet a wise teacher, and are seen for what you are. No book will ask quite the questions that he or she will ask. No book will see beyond the words you speak. Thus it is clear why we might want to convince ourselves that we are better off not relying on a wise teacher. We are afraid that we shall be seen, and that the fixed view that we hold of ourselves will be questioned.

It is possible to start developing a more 'embodied' wisdom by teaching. That will give you a much clearer view of how deep your understanding of the Dharma really goes, especially if those you are teaching are intelligent and self-confident. Ordinary human contact with other members of the spiritual community also has the useful function of challenging us to live out what we know conceptually. It has also the more important function of bringing into consciousness a level of understanding that we had not, perhaps, known we possessed. More important than realizing you do not know what you thought you knew, is realizing that you knew what you did not know you knew.

The qualities that Nāgārjuna says we should look for in a teacher are relatively modest. They should be contented in the sense of being well centred. They should be compassionate in the sense of having a disinterested desire to help others. They should be ethically aware, of course. They should have 'wisdom that can drive out your afflictive emotions,' i.e. not necessarily perfect wisdom. We do not need to sit at the feet of a fully realized master; we need human contact with enough 'embodied' wisdom to enable us to overcome our negative mental states. If we were so fortunate as to spend time with someone who was fully Enlightened, that would indeed be marvellous, but sustained spiritual friendship of the more ordinary kind will really give us everything we need.

Many Westerners have reservations about committing themselves to any cause or any person of a religious nature. There are good reasons for this caution as well as bad ones. One good reason is that a person who is emotionally vulnerable or gullible may be exploited or abused by a charlatan. A bad reason is imagining that by avoiding any kind of commitment we can preserve our spiritual independence. The reliance that Nāgārjuna suggests we place on a teacher should not be understood as dependence in the sense of a passive clinging to the teacher for some kind of emotional security. Reliance on a teacher means taking their advice seriously and trusting their wisdom, but in the end we have to take responsibility for our actions, and not expect the teacher to do everything for us.

Nāgārjuna concludes with a simple, straightforward, and comparatively easy teaching. Wanting to leave the king with something inspiring and, at the same time, well within his capacity to practise, he comes right down to earth. His 'excellent system' begins with speech, for if you are an aspiring Bodhisattva, it is probably through speech that you will make your first contact with the beings you want to help. We should say what is truly pleasant – that is, what is actually useful – and not necessarily say what people are going to find agreeable. We should speak with a kindly awareness of the hearer and of how they might feel. We should be aware of what we are saying and whether it is really worth saying. Without being glib, we should try to speak convincingly. We should speak methodically and with discretion, not simply at random. And of course we should not run others down or defame them. Finally, we should not simply parrot the words of others, but base what we say on personal experience.

Next comes a series of basic qualities which are mainly concerned with the stabilization of a positive mental state, with the containment of one's energies, and with keeping one's emotions under control. When you are excited and 'bubbly', it can feel quite positive, but in fact at such time your energy is loose and unintegrated. Moreover, if your energy is easily aroused, it is more likely to be reactive, so that excitability is not such a positive state as it may seem. Deceitfulness and procrastination make it difficult for others to like us.

The final precept offered to the king is that he should have contact with spiritually-minded people ('supreme people' in this translation). Nāgārjuna says we should associate only with those who are going to support our practice of the Dharma, and avoid those who might undermine it in any way. For someone who is living in the world, that is obviously a counsel of perfection. But we should maintain contact with spiritual friends, and keep these friendships in good repair. When all else fails, it is spiritual friendship that keeps us going through any difficulties, doubts, or disappointments we may encounter on the path to unexcelled Enlightenment.

NOTES AND REFERENCES

References to *Nāgārjuna* are verse numbers in *Nāgārjuna's Precious Garland: Buddhist Advice for Living and Liberation*, analyzed, translated, and edited by Jeffrey Hopkins, Snow Lion Publications, 2007, Part Two, 'Precious Garland of Advice for a King'.

1   *Nāgārjuna*, verse 2.

2   ibid., verse 3.

3   The Tibetan Wheel of Life depicts six realms of existence: those of human beings, gods, *asuras* or anti-gods, animals, hell-beings, and *pretas* or hungry ghosts. According to tradition, one can be born into any of these realms, but once the karma that resulted in one's birth into a particular realm is exhausted, one may be reborn into another. This teaching is taken literally by some Buddhists, metaphorically or psychologically by others. For more information see, for example, Kulananda, *The Wheel of Life*, Windhorse Publications, 2000.

4   *Nāgārjuna*, verses 143–5.

5   ibid., verse 4.

6   ibid., verse 7.

7   ibid., verses 275–82.

8   *Ariyapariyesanā Sutta, Majjhima Nikāya* i.168.

9   *Nāgārjuna*, verse 287.

10 ibid., verses 22–3.

11 ibid., verses 130–2.

12 Romans 12:20.

13 *Nāgārjuna*, verse 21.

14 ibid., verses 174–5.

15 ibid., verse 133.

16 ibid., verses 8–9.

17 The ten precepts are described in several places in the Pāli canon. See Sangharakshita, *The Ten Pillars of Buddhism*, Windhorse Publications, 1996, pp.22–9.

18 *Nāgārjuna*, verses 171–2.

19 ibid., verse 173.

20 The mindfulness of breathing or *ānāpānasati* is one of the most widely-practised meditations in Buddhism. For more details of this meditation and the *mettā bhāvanā*, see, for example, Kamalashila, *Meditation: The Buddhist Way of Tranquillity and Insight*, Windhorse Publications, 1996 or Bodhipaksa, *Wildmind: A Step-by-Step Guide to Meditation*, Windhorse Publications, 2003.

21 *Nāgārjuna*, verses 283–5.

22 Sangharakshita (trans.), *Dhammapada*, Windhorse Publications, 2001, verse 100.

23 *Dhammapada*, verse 1.

24 *Vinaya Culavagga* chapter 7; see also Bhikkhu Ñāṇamoli, *The Life of the Buddha*, Buddhist Publication Society, Kandy 1984, p.263.

25 *Aṅguttara Nikāya* v.342. This is one of several suttas more commonly called the *Mettā Sutta*.

26 *Dhammapada* op. cit., verses 137–40.

27 *Nāgārjuna*, verse 286.

28 ibid., verse 370.

29 ibid., verses 256–64.

30 From the sevenfold puja recited at centres of the Friends of the Western Buddhist Order. This verse is a rendition of chapter 3, verses 20–1, of the *Bodhicaryāvatāra*.

31 *Nāgārjuna*, verses 289–90.

32 ibid., verses 307–17.

33 Romans 31:1.

34 *Nāgārjuna*, verses 148, 150, 169–70.

35 ibid., verse 8.

36 ibid., verses 134–5.

37 ibid., verse 15.

38 ibid., verses 140–2.

39 ibid., verse 9.

40 *Sāmaññaphala Sutta, Dīgha Nikāya* i.54.

41 See *Apaṇṇaka Sutta, Majjhima Nikāya* 60 (especially i.403–4).

42 *Nāgārjuna*, verses 43–5.

43 ibid., verse 46.

44 ibid., verses 47–51.

45 ibid., verses 56–7.

46 ibid., verses 11–13.

47 ibid., verse 10.

48 ibid., verses 146–7.

49 ibid., verse 16.

50 *Lady Windermere's Fan*, act 3.

51 *Nāgārjuna*, verse 77.

52 ibid., verse 288.

53 ibid., verse 24.

54 Psalms 37:35.

55 *Nāgārjuna*, verse 7.

56 ibid., verses 401–3.

57 For more details, see Sangharakshita, *The Taste of Freedom*, Windhorse Publications, 1997.

58 These are listed by Nāgārjuna in verses 403–33, but scholars disagree over how fifty-seven unskilful mental states can be enumerated. For a discussion see Jeffrey Hopkins, op. cit., p.149.

59 *Nāgārjuna*, verses 406–12.

60 *Aṅgulimāla Sutta, Majjhima Nikāya* 86.

61 William Blake, 'The Marriage of Heaven and Hell'.

62 'Reverence … is only excitable in man towards ideal truths which are always mysteries to the understanding.' from 'Table Talk' in *The Complete Works of Samuel Taylor Coleridge*, Harper & Brothers, 1853, p.454.

63 *Nāgārjuna*, verses 413–5.

64 ibid., verses 17–18.

65 Trans. Kate Crosby and Andrew Skilton, *The Bodhicaryāvatāra*, Windhorse Publications, 2002, chapter 6, verse 81.

66 *Nāgārjuna*, verses 416–22.

67 *Dhammapada* op. cit., verse 121.

68 *Nāgārjuna*, verses 425–7.

69 The five *nivaraṇas* or hindrances.

70 *Nāgārjuna*, verses 428–39.

71 These are the core teachings of Buddhism. The Four Noble Truths were expounded by the Buddha in his first major pronouncement after his Enlightenment, the *Dhammacakkappavattana Sutta* (*Saṃyutta Nikāya* 56:11), and comprise (1) the truth of the existence of suffering, (2) the truth of the cause of suffering, which is egotistical desire and craving, (3) the truth of the cessation of suffering, which is the cessation of egotistical desire, and (4) the truth of the way to the cessation of suffering known as the Noble Eightfold Path. The Three Jewels are the main objects of devotion for Buddhists of all schools: the Buddha, the Dharma, and the Sangha. See page 155.

72 *Nāgārjuna*, verse 14.

73 ibid., verse 18.

74 ibid., verses 19–20.

75 Both these terms are used to describe the goal of the spiritual life, effecting complete liberation from cyclic existence. The word *nirvāṇa* literally means extinguished. The word *śūnyatā* (*suññatā* in Pāli) first occurs in what is probably the oldest section of any Buddhist text, the *Pārāyanavagga* of the *Sutta-Nipāta*, where the Buddha tells a layman, Mogharāja, to see the world as empty in order to escape Māra, the king of death. However, it is in the texts of the Mahāyāna schools that the doctrine of *śūnyatā* is fully developed, and it is the principal subject of the Prajñāpāramitā (Perfection of Wisdom) *sūtras* and the writings of the Madhyamaka school.

76 *Nāgārjuna*, verses 299–300.

77 ibid., verses 372–7.

78 Tennyson, *In Memoriam* lxxxiv.

79 *Nāgārjuna*, verses 487–500.

index

WINDHORSE PUBLICATIONS

Windhorse Publications is a Buddhist charitable company based in the UK. We place great emphasis on producing books of high quality that are accessible and relevant to those interested in Buddhism at whatever level. We are the main publisher of the works of Sangharakshita, the founder of the Triratna Buddhist Order and Community. Our books draw on the whole range of the Buddhist tradition, including translations of traditional texts, commentaries, books that make links with contemporary culture and ways of life, biographies of Buddhists, and works on meditation.

As a not-for-profit enterprise, we ensure that all surplus income is invested in new books and improved production methods, to better communicate Buddhism in the 21st Century. We welcome donations to help us continue our work - to find out more, go to www.windhorsepublications.com.

The Windhorse is a mythical animal that flies over the earth carrying on its back three precious jewels, bringing these invaluable gifts to all humanity: the Buddha (the 'awakened one') his teaching, and the community of all his followers.

Windhorse Publications   Perseus Distribution   Windhorse Books
169 Mill Road   1094 Flex Drive   PO Box 574
Cambridge CB1 3AN UK   Jackson TN 38301   Newtown NSW 2042
info@windhorsepublications.com   USA   Australia

TRIRATNA BUDDHIST COMMUNITY

Windhorse Publications is a part of the Triratna Buddhist Community, which has more than sixty centres on five continents. Through these centres, members of the Triratna Buddhist Order offer classes in meditation and Buddhism, from an introductory to deeper levels of commitment. Bodywork classes such as yoga, Tai chi, and massage are also taught at many Triratna centres. Members of the Triratna community run retreat centres around the world, and the Karuna Trust, a UK fundraising charity that supports social welfare projects in the slums and villages of South Asia.

Many Triratna centres have residential spiritual communities and ethical Right Livelihood businesses associated with them. Arts activities are encouraged too, as is the development of strong bonds of friendship between people who share the same ideals. In this way Triratna is developing a unique approach to Buddhism, not simply as a set of techniques, but as a creatively directed way of life for people living in the modern world.

If you would like more information about Triratna please visit www.thebuddhistcentre.com or write to:

London Buddhist Centre   Aryaloka   Sydney Buddhist Centre
51 Roman Road   14 Heartwood Circle   24 Enmore Road
London E2 0HU   Newmarket NH 03857   Sydney NSW 2042
UK   USA   Australia

ALSO FROM WINDHORSE PUBLICATIONS

TRANSFORMING SELF AND WORLD (new edition)
THEMES FROM THE SUTRA OF GOLDEN LIGHT

by Sangharakshita

The *Sutra of Golden Light* has captured imaginations and ignited ideas for centuries but remains as mysterious as it is beautiful. With skill and clarity, Sangharakshita translates the images and episodes of the scripture providing an exploration filled with practical insights. Retaining the potent magic of the original sutra, he shows how this ancient text can help us through a range of contemporary issues such as ecology and economics, culture, morality and government while all the time showing that if we wish to change the world, the most important step we can take is to start with ourselves.

ISBN 9781 899579 95 2
£10.99/$17.95/€13.95
240 pages